Praise for *Out There in the Dark*

"Katharine Coldiron's iconoclastic critical gaze and decadent prose alchemize cinema and autobiography into a book as vivid and resonant as the classic films within. *Out There in the Dark* is a hybrid wonder, a must."
—Henry Hoke, author of *Open Throat*

"*Out There in the Dark* is jargon-free, provocative, persuasive, and insightful. The critical intelligence in the imaginative position: this is what Katharine Coldiron deploys to a remarkable degree and across an impressively wide range of material."
—David Shields, author of *Reality Hunger*

"Katharine Coldiron's essays are a marvelous combination of personal and pop cultural reflections, seen through the lens of the films she's loved. *Out There in the Dark* threads its way somewhere between Roland Barthes and Emily Nussbaum, resulting in a collection that is thoughtful, trenchant, and keenly observed."
—Elizabeth Gonzalez James, author of *The Bullet Swallower*

"A luminous object lesson in how we create our selves out of our experience of art, in the meaning that making meaning out of art can make out of our lives, Katharine Coldiron's *Out There in the Dark* is surprising and moving, whether it's taking on *Apocalypse Now* or *Alien from L.A.* Sometimes mournful, sometimes ecstatic, always insightful and personal, Coldiron's hybrid essays are a joy to read and think through."
—Gabriel Blackwell, author of *Madeleine E.* and *Doom Town*

Out There in the Dark

Katharine Coldiron

Autofocus Books
Easton, Pennsylvania

Published by Autofocus Books
autofocusbooks.com

Essays/Literature
ISBN: 978-1-957392-37-0
Library of Congress Control Number: 2025931913

Cover design by Amy Wheaton
Cover image: "Zootropo" from *El Mundo Físico*, 1882, uploaded to Flickr by Fondo Antiguo de la Biblioteca de la Universidad de Sevilla, edited and retouched by Amy Wheaton

Out There in the Dark

For Rick Blackwood, who started the fire,
and Christopher Higgs, who stoked the hell out of it

Hollywood is very powerful, and very real. No matter how make-believe it is, it is real, and it moves and shakes and it is not something to mess around with.

Wendy vanden Heuvel in Jean Stein's *West of Eden*

You see, this is my life. It always will be. There's nothing else—just us, and the cameras, and those wonderful people out there in the dark.

Sunset Boulevard

Contents

Author's Note

Three hundred words into the first essay in this book, I mention Plato's allegory of the cave. In regular life, I joke that every intro to film class in the country either starts or should start there. That's more or less why I chose to start there, too, because this is a book about film and about me in equal measures.

Pretend, asks Plato, that a group of people have been chained inside a cave all their lives, restrained so they can see nothing except the wall in front of them, not even each other. People outside the cave project images against the wall using fire and puppetry. The prisoners believe that the images are reality, because they know nothing else.

As an allegory, it's loose enough to apply to multiple concepts—Plato's point was about relying on our senses rather than reason and intellect to interpret the world—but it's extremely on the nose for film studies. The shadow play on the cave wall is, changing *solely* technological development since 400 BC, a movie in a theater. Unlike Plato's prisoners, though, cinemagoers enter the cave willingly, with full knowledge that the screen is not reality. At present, we come and go frequently from the cave, living life beyond the simulation and then voluntarily imprisoning ourselves within it (most of us daily, via television). Plato, grump that he is, would find this morally unsound; he would want us all to put down our phones and touch grass.

But I am happiest, most lucid, in the cave. In understanding the shadow play on that wall, I understand the one that goes on inside my head, where memories degrade to colors and emotions, where interactions lose specificity until I only know it happened on a sunny day or in a Starbucks. I can use what I've seen to make sense of what I don't know: I see Martin Sheen cutting a brutal, surreal path through a shitty war, and I can pin it to the empty spaces of what my father won't tell me. I study the layers of trickery between actresses speaking and singing for each other in 1950s musicals, and it helps me sort out what truth means to me.

I don't know what I would make of my life if I didn't have these tools.

We live encased, in our skulls and our meat bodies and under our roofs. Film takes place between the eye and the mind, an electric circuit that closes easily. I shut my eyes right now and I can see everything in this book: the von Trapp children walking down the stairs in *The Sound of Music*; Robert Duvall crouching amid yellow smoke in *Apocalypse Now*; Debbie Reynolds dancing in *Singin' in the Rain*; Marilyn Monroe screaming at the men she loves in *The Misfits*; Orson Welles walking between an infinite pair of mirrors in *Citizen Kane*; Meryl Streep standing at the podium to accept her Oscar for *Sophie's Choice*; Maria Schneider crossing a street in *Last Tango in Paris*; Joan Crawford slapping her child in *Mildred Pierce*; Delphine Seyrig peeling potatoes in *Jeanne Dielman, 23, quai du Commerce, 1080 Bruxelles.*

These men and women are strangers, positioned to entertain us, but I know them as I know my own arms and legs. Their images cohere in the darkness behind my eyes as easily as images of my father's smile, my mother's hands. The time in which critics did not take film seriously as an art form is over, but I feel that we have not yet truly reckoned with how entwined with media our (humans', but especially Americans') emotional lives became by the end of the 20th century. I have tried, on my own. The results follow.

(Perhaps Plato has already performed this reckoning, telling us to permit no simulations in the Republic; they too easily trick and harm us. Perhaps Walter Benjamin intended not to inform us, but to warn us. Perhaps Jean Baudrillard hoped to be theoretical rather than descriptive.

Perhaps it is too late to listen to philosophers.)

Other writers make sense of their lives with plainer prose, or more reasonable tools. *Tell all the truth but tell it slant*, Emily Dickinson advises, and her words have been solace to me as I essay (assay). I do not know how to write a genuine, unslant human truth. I needed lists, diagrams, fiction, research, and the words of others to assemble this project, this working-out of things that have happened to me. And no matter the textual strategy, I return always to film.

All this is to say: what follows is not a book of film essays or lyric essays or speculative memoir or autofiction or anything else easy to slap a call number on. It's all that, chopped and screwed. I myself would prefer if my writing was more categorizable, if I could arrange my thoughts in a less patchwork manner. But it is not. My brain has never worked like that.

Yet it has always porously adhered to film, since I was a tiny girl watching the Star Wars trilogy on Betamax. I loved books, but books told other people's stories. Movies told the stories I wanted to live. The stories I *have* lived only come into focus when I project them on the wall, and when I line up a second moving image over the first—the movie over the memory forms a three-dimensional experience.

I see light best through celluloid. Or maybe not *best*; maybe *most usefully.* In grad school I tried to look at myself through the houses I've lived in, and it was a painful experiment. Physically locating my life showed me how transitory it had been, how easily dis-located. Movies can screen almost anywhere, can offer the same emotional experience in any place. Stories like the ones in this book can light up any dark room, as long as I have a projector, an empty wall, and an audience. Always an audience. Without that, the circuit remains closed, the electricity circling without release.

Storytelling, I have averred elsewhere, is the most powerful way to keep ourselves from the void. Human beings have been gathering around fires to tell stories since the dawn of our intelligence. I believe that, and it's sacred to me.

The projector is my fire. For you, I light it up.

The Girl on the Bike

In 1965, the actors playing the von Trapp children march down the split staircase of their house. They march noisily in time with tweets from Captain von Trapp's whistle. The camera follows them, step by step, down the stairs, into the large foyer until they march in place, presented in a line for their new governess. Their chests and chins shove forward. Their arms swing. They stop and right-face. Brigitta, lost in a book, wanders in and finds her tardy place in the line, a place left empty for her all the way down the stairs and into the foyer.

These actors are fixed in time and space. They performed this action in life a limited number of times (several takes, perhaps) and then they were finished performing it, but their shadows will go on marching down the staircase in theaters, VCRs, Blu-Ray players, data streams, synapses until *The Sound of Music* passes out of human knowledge.

Look at them. Down the stairs they go, again. And again. In 1965, in 1972, in 1981, in 1994, in 2008, in 2015, in 2027, in 2033, and so on for the foreseeable future. Down the stairs, and down the stairs again. It has happened before, and it will happen again, in places and contexts unfathomed. In an Ohio basement. In a Moscow movie-house. In a shack in Texas. In a mansion in Seattle. On a tiny cold-adapted television in Antarctica as a treat for the visitors on Christmas. In Sweden. In Kenya. In Beijing. Everywhere.

Down the stairs. They move, and are affixed in a single place; they breathe and live, and are trapped in a single moment.

They are two-dimensional, three-dimensional, and four-dimensional at once.

This, then, is immortality.

*

First, we must understand cinema as movement through space and time.

First, we must consider Plato's allegory of the cave. The watchers of shadows on the wall are cinema-goers. (Do they *elect* to be fooled by simulacra? Or are they naïve enough for such pale trickery to work on them?)

First, we must realize that every frame of every film is the result of a thousand choices.

First, we must recognize our removal from the machinations of the shadows. The screen stands between us and the internal world depicted on it. There is no communion.

(Between thee and me, reader, there is communion. I have made a thousand choices to bring you here, but the walls between us are mere paper and cardboard and ink. I strain to touch you. There, or there. Are you allergic to me? Scratch your skin.)

First, we must accept the fundamental fakery of cinema.

First, we must believe the Wizard: he is great and powerful, and he is a flimflam artist: both.

First, we must know what we enter when we face the cave wall.

*

Put yourself in a car, driving to work down a suburban street in the San Fernando Valley: four to five lanes, brisk 40 MPH speed limit, trees and houses on either side. The sketchy 7-11 is coming up on your left. The church that sometimes actually has decent life advice on its marquee was back there on the right. A couple of the houses on this street are terminally being worked on, enclosed by fencing and unfinished-looking. Before one of them is an older woman holding the leash of a small fluffy dog. You drive by at 40 MPH, so you don't see everything, but flashes linger: the woman's stance (bent slightly forward), the ferociousness of the little dog, barking inconsolably, the tautness of the stretched leash. It was a Bichon Frise, maybe, and her shirt was pink, maybe, over jean shorts with barrel-width openings.

A few seconds down the street, you drive by a girl on a bicycle. Flashes: it's a lady's bicycle, the kind that forces one to sit up regally instead of hunching over handlebars placed parallel to the ground. The girl is not a girl, not yet a woman—maybe twenty, give or take. She carries a gray messenger bag slung across her back. It shifts to and fro as she pedals, which must be annoying.

The girl on the bike is riding toward the Bichon. The Bichon is barking in the direction of the girl on the bike. You're fairly certain that the humans in this tableau are obstructed from seeing each other, because of the hedges that protrude into the sidewalk, the construction fences, and so forth. You could see the barking dog, and the bike, and know that one is reacting to the other. You could predict what would happen when the two trajectories met. The dog would bark and bark, working itself into a frenzy, and the dog's owner would shout and yank on its leash and holler inaudible apologies to the girl on the bike as she rode by. But neither of the two participants in this waltz (three, if you count the dog) could see it coming at the time you could.

You feel like God. You feel like you are peering at ants. Yet you feel impotent: you cannot alter or affect the collision of these two (or three) parties, even if you can see it coming. You giggle at the comedy of dog on leash, girl on bike, and riding by before the thunder but after the lightning, all morning, but you cannot connect it to the bell of meaning that strikes in you, considering the God's-eye view, until you remember the von Trapp children.

*

I invent two people, a woman and a man. I call the woman Beth and the man Spencer. I don't know anyone by these names. I find it easier to make up stories about people I don't already know. I know three Melissas, and I don't think I can make one up who has nothing to do with the other three. I need blank slates. Or I need to hide who these characters really are, to save embarrassment. Either way, names can't correspond to real people or it won't work.

Beth hunches in front of a mirror upstairs in her parents' house. She applies mascara. Spencer sits on her parents' sofa, hands possessively covering his knees, clearing his throat about every fifteen seconds. As I write this paragraph, the figures take shape in my mind: they're teenagers headed for a dance. Homecoming, or Prom. Spencer has a crew cut. Beth's dress is trendy and awful. Her parents hover and whisper in the kitchen. I don't like any of this, because it isn't interesting; if I can make up the details this easily, see it so clearly, it's probably pointed in the direction of cliché.

So let's try again. Beth is still upstairs applying mascara, but it's a condo she owns with Spencer, to whom she isn't married. They're going on a date. He stands in the kitchen with a wineglass, trying to slow his heartbeat. I must decide why he's nervous, but I'm stuck, at the moment. I know they will have conflicting motivations at this dinner, and I will tell the reader of them, in this way creating tension that will keep the story humming. For instance, Spencer wants to propose, and Beth wants to confess that she's cheating on him. Or Spencer wants to tell Beth he's bisexual, something he's kept secret for the length of their relationship, while Beth has been hiding for three months that she got a promotion which makes her better paid than he is. If you are informed of these burning secrets before Beth finishes putting her makeup on, before Spencer drinks the last of his wine, you will probably want to keep reading, to see how dinner goes. There will be a climax. There will be a denouement. Something unexpected will happen, like the couple's car hitting a deer, or a hobo, or a child (depending on how perverse I'm feeling) on the way home. And nothing will ever be the same again.

These are two avenues. I may choose a third.

Maybe Spencer sits in his living room, a widower, watching *The Sound of Music* on a rainy night. The hour grows late. Captain von Trapp's whistle tweets. Spencer should have gone to bed even before starting, but he kept saying to himself *just until the next song, just until the next song.* He glances up and Beth walks down the stairs, fastening her watch. He shuts his eyes tight and she walks down the stairs again, stooped, leaning on the rail so hard it creaks. She walks down the stairs, her hair in an updo, her wrist left bare for a corsage. She walks down the stairs wide open and shouting after she guessed the password for his laptop and checked his browser history. She walks down the stairs before they'd ripped up the carpet and then after Belloq scratched the shit out of the new laminate in a fit of nerves. She walks down the stairs and he watches her. He doesn't know all of these Beths, but he knows some of them bones-out. Sometimes she looks at her feet, hunting for the next step, and other times she could be sleepwalking. Spencer watches her and watches her. Down and down and yet down.

That paragraph doesn't come from a writer who lives and dies by Joycean structure, Chekhovian strategy, Freytag's pyramid scheme. I'm not interested in whether Beth is a ghost or Spencer is hallucinating. I followed the sentences, is all. I don't know what it means.

How many times did I walk down the stairs in my Maryland townhouse, where I lived for seven years? I imagine all those descents superimposed on one another, a holograph, me with innumerable Hydra heads, my clothing so varied it's just a brown splotch—like when my mother and I melted all the leftover bits of crayon together. My voice a dull blat, a Babel. I talk on the phone to a dozen people. I call out to my husband or my guests or the mailman.

Who's there? I ask.

Who's there?

*

If Nietzsche is correct, the Bichon Frise and the girl on the bike have met many times and will meet many times again. An infinity of collisions. You will have seen the moment after the lightning but before the thunder an infinity of times, too, but you will never have seen the collision itself. You will remain impotent to alter the outcome of the incident. Driving by—despite seeing down the road a little further than either party—you are *not* God. God can alter; Cassandra can only see. Both have witnessed enough patterns to understand their outcomes, but one is a playwright and the other is an actress. Cassandra has read the script but she must play her part. Which is, I think, why she coaxes all the Greek women into suicide.

Cassandra should have been a writer.

When a dog barks at a bike down the street, will one inevitably topple to the other? Or is that not snappy enough to be a koan?

*

Here's another thing I know about Joycean short stories: the writer can duck out before anyone has to do any hard work. Consider upper-middle-class Beth and Spencer, at a dim and tony restaurant on the brink of drastic confessions. If I were writing this story, I would pick one of them to unload his/her secrets, and the other party would hold her/his tongue to salvage the relationship. In life, the one who kept her/his mouth shut would almost certainly live to regret it, and the relationship would go in the toilet anyway. But in the story, this person will evanesce into netherfiction before the consequences slam into her, truckload-heavy and long visible. We end on that breathless harmony of tension, sacrifice, secrets, rather than coping with the low, slow tuba line of separating his kitchenware from hers while the moving truck idles outside.

Life and its consequences have little to do with the consequences in a conventional short story, which must bear two characteristics: they must be inevitable (the only way the story could have ended) and unexpected (the reader never saw it coming). The best traditional stories achieve this and they are lovely. Veer too hard to starboard, and the story's predictable; too hard to port, and the story's confusing. As if a football careened out of left field. It's not easy to strike this balance, which is why so many stories are either confusing or predictable. The good ones leave you trailing along after the characters, wanting to know what happens next, like a toddler whose parent is trying to leave him at daycare.

As an experiment, imagine for yourself what a character undergoes after the story concludes. You may have done this many times, but let's try it anyway. If you pretend that *The Sound of Music* is not based on a true story, and that Maria is young and beautiful and Georg Von T. is a silver fox, and they take the kids into the Alps to escape the Nazis, well, what then? Do they arrive in Switzerland still beautifully dressed, in their lederhosen and colorful head-scarves, clear-eyed and well-nourished?

No. They do not. The kids complain the whole way there. Gretel has to be carried most of the time, and only Liesl agrees to help Maria and Georg with this burden. There's some bodily unpleasantness; for instance, one morning Kurt takes a handful of his own waste and menaces Louisa with it. She falls and cuts her shin quite badly, and her limping slows them all down. Maria is vomiting most of the way there and ultimately miscarries. There is never enough to eat; swallowing snow to keep hydrated leaves their faces numb and their teeth hurting; and they run out of matches only a quarter of the way into their journey.

You'd prefer to think of them singing their way to freedom, I know, but that's why the story ends where it does. The reality of a journey across the Alps with seven children makes for poor fiction and even poorer Hollywood.

Climb ev'ry mountain.

I'm not trying to ruin *The Sound of Music* for you. I'm trying to note that stories are stories and life is life and there ain't much leeway there. But the tension between the two remains an interesting contact zone. Sometimes, in life, the ending is inevitable but unexpected. The real von Trapps really did cross the Alps, after all. (On a train.)

*

Now that we have faced the cave wall with open eyes.

Now that we have accepted its limitations.

Now that we have erased Freytag's triangle.

Now that we have dispensed with the story about Prom Night and the story about upper-middle-class dinner tensions.

Now that we know reality and truth to be distinct.

Now that I have reached out for your hand in the dark, pointed and said *you*, implicated your existence in this narrative.

Now that the Wizard is out from behind the curtain.

Now.

*

Beth walks down the stairs. She cannot do this in two dimensions. It takes you time to read those words; the language takes up space on the page. Whether I invented her or not is beside the point. Her existence is only as concrete as yours, love, because you're not sitting here with me as I write these words, and she is. She walked down the stairs several hundred words ago, and now she does it again. I can tell you what's in her mind and heart, and it'll be up to you to conjure her, as I am conjuring you. It may not be worth it. You may be better off with a movie. May I suggest *The Sound of Music*?

Here we sit together in front of the movie screen. The actors play their parts. I've seen this before, so I know what happens. Poor Baroness Schrader. If only I could stop the car and go back and tell the woman with the dog to hang out in someone's yard and kneel to keep a tight hold on the dog while the girl on the bike rides by. But behind the safety glass of my windows, beyond the impassable scrim of screen between me and 1965, I am powerless.

With you, this is not so. With you, I am not Cassandra; I am God.

Beth walks down the stairs. There is no Spencer in this version of her story; not yet. She walks outside. She gets her bike out of the garage. The air in early morning smells of dust and smog and slight moisture. Citysmell. She gets on the bike. She pedals down the street. A blue SUV passes her, going in the opposite direction, just before she hears a dog up ahead, barking, barking, barking inconsolably.

Charlie Don't Surf

Duvall hates the scene. The soliloquy of it, the speechy quality, pisses him off, rankles him in a way he can't place until the first take. One of the PFCs watching him, face off-camera, tugs a corner of his mouth up and back, rapid as a blink, after a particular line. A fellow actor, unconvinced.

Two more takes and he says to Coppola that it isn't working, he knows it isn't, and he needs the night to turn it over. They shoot some more beach shit, set-ups, so they don't lose the day.

In the dank, dirty hotel, he speaks the words again and again into the bathroom mirror. *I love the smell of napalm in the morning. I love the smell of napalm in the morning. I love the smell of napalm in the morning.* They piss him off, still. Not just because they made that PFC smirk for a fraction of a moment. Not just because they made him look demanding, prissy, in front of the crew. Not that. Not that. Some other.

I love the smell of napalm in the morning.

It's impossible to act this scene well, he mutters, and thus, clarity.

*

One night, lying in my bunk bed, I imagined my father's death. It was not a realistic scenario. I saw him on the deck of a sort of generic boat, midway between a wooden sailing ship and a compact, modern Coast Guard-type vessel, neither of which resembled the ships he actually commanded, navigated, lived on for six to nine months out of the year. His ships were gray metal, scaled so massively that they dwarfed men to toothpicks at parade rest. They maintained high population, crowded decks. A man would not stand on the deck alone, nor would he, in any possibility, die the way I pictured it.

My mind set him on the deck of this unlikely ship in his weekend attire of bootcut jeans and a soft cotton oxford shirt, instead of the summer khakis or dress whites I'd seen on him thousands of times. He stood with arms spread wide, his limbs dancing, a large, neat circle carved out of his torso. A cannonball, a literal cannonball, like from a colonial-era cannon, had just sliced through him.

This scene looped itself for minutes, hours. He never fell, and the hole in his chest never filled in.

Roger Coldiron dead, I told myself. *Roger Coldiron dead.* It became a quiet frenzy in me, a bleeding gash in my palm that I rubbed and rubbed. I sought the bottom of the pain, the place where the emotional truth of my father's death lay.

I worked myself up so thoroughly that I started crying. I crawled down from my bunk bed, opened my door, tiptoed across the creaky hall, and crept into my parents' room.

The covers, humped and adult-sized, shifted. The TV flashed mutely.

Roger, said my mother in a muddy, sleepish voice. Roger. It's Kate. Kate's here.

The covers shifted some more. My father asked what was wrong.

I said I was worried about burglars breaking in. I don't know why. While that did worry me sometimes, what had gotten me out of bed and down the hall was imagining him dead, and somehow I couldn't tell him this. It seemed insulting, like it was rude to tell my father I'd considered his mortality.

And this I remember: he sighed. A long, deep sigh. He didn't get out of their bed or invite me into it. He reassured me in a fashion I no longer remember—probably with logic and likelihood, that was more his speed than genuine comfort—and told me to go back to sleep.

I had not been asleep.

I went back to my room and climbed up into the bunk bed and turned over the tape of Anne Murray in the little black cassette player I kept up there and pressed play. I think my mother might have come a little later on to comfort me for real, but I might have invented that idea.

Once I told this story and a friend asked if they had been having sex. Once another friend asked if I'd ever walked in on my parents having sex and I remembered this story. I don't know if they were having sex. I don't have a specific memory of what the covers were doing, and I didn't see flesh or movement that I remember. I'm not sure it matters. A parent should not sigh heavily when his child needs comfort, no matter what she's interrupted him doing.

*

Lorrie Stirm is 15 in the picture. Both her platform shoes have left the ground. Hands and arms reaching as wide as she can make them. Her father, back to the camera, wears a uniform, shoes, and a haircut that could come from any time, any era of military engagement. His family's appearance, not his, marks the era. His sons sport shaggy, grown-out moptops, and his wife has pantyhose and an oval helmet of hair. Lorrie's broad collar and corduroy miniskirt decide the matter. This is March 17, 1973, toward the end of US military involvement in Vietnam, and Lt. Col. Robert Stirm reaches hesitantly for his family: two daughters, two sons, wife.

Lorrie is closest of the group to her father. Per the captured energy in the photo, the children run while the adults walk. Cindy, the younger sister, wears a truly stupid outfit, with Mary Janes, knee socks, and a lacy pinafore, poor girl. Roger, younger son, looks like he has on a windbreaker, a long collar tab poking out of it. That morning, the children and their mother woke up and dressed to meet Lt. Col. Stirm, who'd been in captivity in Vietnam since October of 1967. They decided what to wear that morning based on the event of the day. Lorrie picked out a sweater and brushed her hair. Loretta took her massive corsage out of the fridge and pinned it on. *We're going to see him again,* their minds hummed. *We're going to see him again.*

I know these mornings. I know the car ride, the nervous energy buzzing louder than the radio. I know parking among dozens, hundreds of cars filled with dependents. Feeling inadequate because I'm carrying nothing: no posterboard with a hand-markered message or family joke, no Mylar balloons, no bouquet of flowers. Knowing without asking that such totems would be a waste of money, not what my father would want from us.

"Why do we get dressed up?" I asked my mother once.

"Because your father deserves to see us looking our best," she replied.

"But he hasn't seen us in six months," I said. "He'd like to see us in burlap sacks. As long as it's us. Why does he care what we're wearing?"

"It's better to look nice," she said. "Even better than seeing us is seeing us pretty."

I found this extremely weird, and dumb, and I hated dresses venomously, so I grumbled until it became obvious that Mom wasn't changing her mind.

Now, as an adult, I understand that social customs demand

dressing up for certain occasions, such as greeting the patriarch after a deployment. But, at a philosophical level, I still can't quite see the point. Presumably it matters even less what his wife wears if he hasn't seen her in six months, because all he can see is his wife, her face and her smile, the woman he married and the child she made with him. The outfit she fretted over is thoroughly beside the point.

Or maybe it does matter. Did Lt. Col. Stirm see his family's clothes? Did he notice the makeup Loretta carefully applied? Did he care that they didn't have posterboard and flowers? They had five years to acquire such gifts, but all they brought was themselves.

Sometimes, after the initial greeting, Mom and I would go up on the ship with Dad, see his crewmates, drink bug juice from the wardroom, look at his stateroom. The tiny bed, the poster of Yoda's best wisdom. The steep ladder-stairs between decks, not built for a child to navigate. I do not know why he wanted to take us on the ship instead of allowing us to take him home. Home. Home with us, his wife and child.

*

I watch *Apocalypse Now* for the first time in five years. My body recoils against it. My skin doesn't fit; my eyes itch; my fingers move, restless.

It's a masterpiece, of course. I knew that when I first saw it, unexpectedly, in high school (we were reading *Heart of Darkness*). I have thought so every time I've seen it. The pacing is odd, characters appear out of nowhere and disappear again, we don't know where food or water is coming from, it's impossible to remember in what order the events of the film occur—and these are all features, not bugs. The weirdness of *Apocalypse Now* is part of what makes it brilliant. Few other films so blankly present war for what it is: surreal, pointlessly violent, restless, hysterical, full of extraordinary men seen once and never again.

Coppola said he wanted to take the audience "through an unprecedented experience of war and have them react as much as those who had gone through the war." So I'm not nuts in feeling traumatized, re-traumatized, utterly overcome by the experience of this film.

I can feel my insides vibrating during Lt. Col. Kilgore's scenes. The way Duvall stands, strides, touches his crotch, speaks to his men, it's smooth and charismatic and fearsome. He makes the film anarchic, frightening. This is how they look, men who make war. Whether he is one, or is acting as one extremely well, is anyone's guess.

My father had a different voice when he was with men, or work colleagues, than he did at home with me and Mom. It was deeper and louder, more prone to laughter. I only heard it a few times. I don't know if it was his real voice or if his real voice was the one I heard at home.

Airborne, Sheen murmurs.

This high school experience with *Apocalypse Now* was not the first time I'd seen a Vietnam movie. That was *Forrest Gump*, which I saw in the theater with my father. As soon as the first scene with Forrest actually in Vietnam began (Gary Sinise strides through camp shirtless, chewing a cigar; generally the scene owes a lot to Coppola and Duvall), I tensed. I tried to stretch out supernatural feelers to my father to see if he was okay, if he needed to leave. He sat there, betraying nothing. Later, I noticed that the GIs in the film carried their cigarettes on their helmets, anchored by an elastic strap. I dared to lean over and ask my father: "Did they really do that?"

"Yes," he said. "You'd keep your toilet paper up there too,

to keep it dry."

That is one of three things he has ever said in my presence about his time in Vietnam.

I know that he was a corpsman with the Navy who was attached to a platoon of Marines. I know, based on his age, that he was there sometime during the 1970s. I know that he saw bad deaths and that he almost won the Silver Star for something. That's about all. He has said next to nothing, and I don't think it's kind to ask.

All the guys in *Forrest Gump*, all the guys in *Platoon*, all the guys in *Full Metal Jacket* and *The Deer Hunter*, they could all be my father. All of them. Any of them. Not that I think Hollywood gets Vietnam totally right, because films are imitation, not war. But I am haunted by those actors in camouflage, sweating and smoking and bleeding. I don't know enough about what my father did and saw to know what applies to him and what doesn't. All of it aches in me, as if I have new bones that hurt for what he might have gone through. Was he in the shit? Did he kill people? Did he go to Cambodia or Da Nang or Fort Bragg, California? I do not know. I may never know. I know that he suffered, that he still suffers.

I watch *Apocalypse Now* not more than twice a decade. As a work of art, it bowls me over every time, but I still can't stand to watch it too often. It's a visceral film, its madness a swinging axe missing you by a few millimeters each time. And the fact that any of these men could be him, the man who played basketball with me and taught me how to ski using physics and explained the shades of Mutually Assured Destruction in the car one day, makes it too hard to watch, despite its profound merits.

*

The week before Lt. Col. Stirm faced his family on the runway, Loretta wrote him a letter to say she wanted a divorce. What a cold woman, you might say, to dump her POW husband immediately before he returns home. But if you have not been a military wife, reader, judge not. It's a difficult life.

The Stirms did divorce and Loretta remarried. The following year, Lt. Col. Stirm gave an interview to *People* about the financial details of his divorce so full of bitterness and fury that I ached to read it. "All those dreams I had in prison were nothing but dust," he said to the reporter. "I've been taken to the cleaners."

Loretta, after receiving what was owed her under the law as a military spouse, seems to have retreated into private life. The picture of her and her children greeting Lt. Col. Stirm on the runway lives on. It sits in history books, testament to a confusing 20th century war and the people who survived it. She and her family members all display the photograph in their homes, according to *Smithsonian*, except for Lt. Col. Stirm. He does not.

It's called *Burst of Joy*, that photograph. Sal Veder won a Pulitzer for it. Lorrie and her broad collar will show up in textbooks for decades to come. Loretta and her smile and her gigantic corsage. And the back of Lt. Col. Stirm's head. Whatever is in his mind, whatever could be written on his face, is not part of the picture. If he is thinking of the captivity from which he was rescued, the deprivation and the boredom and the terror; if he is thinking of the three-day-old letter from Loretta; if he is thinking of the daughter running toward him with love in every inch of her body—all that is spooled up under his hat and inaccessible. The photograph cannot tell us.

Where did they go, the Stirm family, after this picture was taken? Did they go out somewhere for a meal, or did they drive home? What did they talk about in the car? How did Loretta tell her children that their father was going away again?

In its most basic interpretation, *Burst of Joy* depicts a homecoming. A soldier returns to his family. But that family is soon to eject him. "Home," then, has no meaning for Lt. Col. Stirm, even as he's standing on that runway, becoming, in a shutter-click, a poster boy for the word. He's coming *back*, not home. Home is illusory. As anonymous as the back of his head, and as incommunicative. As fake as a movie set.

*

The more they tried to make it just like home, the more they made everybody miss it, Sheen narrates. Everything about the Vietnam illustrated in *Apocalypse Now* is false, constructed. It's not even Vietnam, it's the Philippines. It's 1976 or 1977, and the war is over. These are actors. Kurtz isn't real; even Brando edges into the mythical.

Duvall plays the guitar and chews on his cigarette holder. It's a good hat and a pleasant scene, easy to ad-lib. A fire, food, company. He's cheery for a little while, until he remembers the monologue he has to try again once the sun's up. He thinks he's got a strategy: don't *act* it. Zip up into the skin of Kilgore and feel it around him, comforting, not choking. The cigarette holder helps. A touch of frippery to hold against the body of the man.

He stands up from the fire, towers over the men. Reaches to adjust himself, leaves his hand on his balls a few ticks longer than necessary. That's Kilgore. Power in what makes him a man. Reinforcing itself, swelling on its own worship.

"*Charlie don't surf,*" he bellows. He touches his balls again. Wars start in here, he thinks. Death and fire. Women make life and we make death. I want to go home.

*

My mother and father first separated when I was eight or nine. Those were deployment years, Gulf War years. It's likely that, at least once, my mother and I greeted my returning father at the base with a sense of home as uncertain as Lt. Col. Stirm's.

A military spouse must be unfailingly supportive. But humans fail.

When my mother moved out, my father fell glum and didn't recover until she moved back in again. In my memory he is nearly a stereotype, an Eeyore. Once, in the kitchen, I tried to tell him to snap out of it. "Life goes on!" I exhorted.

"I don't see why," he replied.

I left, fed up with his mopery, but his words frightened me. I don't know if I ever told anyone about that exchange. I don't think I did.

One of the crucial aspects of *Burst of Joy*, according to Sal Veder, is Lt. Col. Stirm's position: back to the camera. He could be any GI at any time in history. The uniform, the haircut. He's a Vietnam POW, but he could be anyone.

That's illogical. The Vietnam war was not like any other. But Lt. Col. Stirm does have an air of anonymity compared to the family, in their chosen clothes. It's as if they're part of a different picture than he is, as if they are prefacing what will happen in a few weeks, when the family splits off into their own pictures. Their own homes.

My father lives in his own home and I live in mine, a few thousand miles away. We haven't spoken in years. The last time we did, I found him as bitter as oversteeped tea—as bitter as Lt. Col. Stirm in that *People* interview. I don't know when he is living, whether it's a time when I wronged him or a time before he'd been wronged by anyone at all, but it's unbearable to hear him that way.

Still I weep at *Apocalypse Now*, at whatever version of that horror my father lived through. Actors macheteing through the jungle in southeast Asia cut too close to the DNA he gave me, to the war and fire he must have seen and stored, that I tiptoed around and wasn't told about my whole life.

The home they made for me was real until it wasn't. It collapsed, like an unhooked backdrop. The picture snapped by Sal Veder on the runway that day, the burst of joy, the promise of homecoming, was real until it wasn't. Home, and Vietnam, both stored in Lt. Col. Stirm's head, and one was realer to Loretta than the other.

He could be any soldier.

*

The camera drifts along the river, tracks a walk through chaos, records everything without blinking or stopping. Music comes and goes, to add as needed, to remind the viewer that organized sound, beyond cacophony, exists. Valkyries sing to heighten the fear and swagger of men. Color and performance and darkness and the whipping movement of copter blades against smoke. The GIs look exhausted, rumpled, too numb or new to be frightened.

The film is a picaresque, I realize, once I stand back enough to see it. A series of adventures laid out in a journey, something linear without meaningful accumulation. The order of events doesn't matter. Kurtz still waits at the end. I know he is coming, but he matters so much less to me than the rest of it: the damp uniforms, the cigarettes, the constant threat, the oppressive sun. The way each man can only arrange himself so many ways on the limited space of the boat before he is sitting how and where he's sat before. The long stretches of nothing and occasional spikes of terror. What waits for these men at home.

I know he must have seen the jungle, seen combat; he told me once, in a fit of despair, that they could've put what was left of his best friend in a Ziploc baggie. But there's a limit to what he has told me, what he will ever tell me. All I can do when I sit in front of *Apocalypse Now* is imagine. And I do: I imagine him in something like this place, at something near this time, doing and seeing terrible acts, all wrapped in spools of magnetic tape behind the forehead I've kissed, behind the eyes that saw me born. I don't know what's really in there. I watch other stories, fictions, and I shiver and look away.

SELL THE HOUSE
SELL THE CAR
SELL THE KIDS
FIND SOMEONE ELSE
FORGET IT!
I'M <u>NEVER</u> COMING ~~HOME~~ BACK
FORGET IT!!!

reads a note from an Army captain to his wife. The captain, a minor character, goes to retrieve Kurtz months before Sheen is sent on the same mission. He's meant to demonstrate Kurtz's capacity for persuasion into madness, but Dennis Hopper performs that duty far better. What wife would read this note and understand? What did Lt. Col. Stirm's letters look like, if he sent any?

How could she have written him a *letter* to tell him their marriage was over?

How could my mother have dolled up and dragged me to the base over and over again without breaking?

Though I love and deeply miss my father, I don't really know him. I realize that when I look at *Burst of Joy* and I see Lt. Col.

Stirm walking away from the camera toward his family. They can't know what he went through during those five years away. He has to live with his memory in a way that no one can touch. He has to know what he saw and did, and I, young and female and distant, do not.

That is a blessing. I don't want to know, the same way I don't want to watch *Apocalypse Now* too often. Yet not knowing keeps me on the outside of whatever his suffering entails. Always looking at the back of his head, at his shined shoes walking away from me.

*

Here's the secret Duvall grips when he squats down to begin speaking: conviction. The belief he carries in his Army-issue trousers that he is where he belongs. That a battlefield can be a home. And as he's been speaking the man, dressing the man, cradling the man's balls, he has grasped another element: erasure. No storage of what he's seen in his mind; the capacity to forget the ugly parts and remember the soaring, grating voice of the chopper's engine.

I love the smell of napalm in the morning.

They will only take it seriously if he takes it seriously. He must weep to make them weep. He must buy into it completely, must be sure and engaged, obliterative with his will.

The smell. You know, that gasoline smell.

And the only way to flatten the enemy is to forget them. Remember nothing. Remember the music and not the screams. Live in the fire and not in the charred corpse.

Smelled like...victory.

Immersed so deeply in Kilgore, Duvall does not move when a shell explodes much closer behind him than it was supposed to. Sheen flinches, and remembers to act a moment later. He stares. The whole set stares.

Someday this war's gonna end.

Bright White American Smile

My teeth keep chipping.

I think it's the porcelain. I think the porcelain is stronger, harder, than what grew out of my jaw when I was a child. The real teeth bang against the porcelain and fail the test.

Eight porcelain teeth form my smile, now. I don't feel very good about this. The bright white American smile is just another Marxist/Gramscian/Foucauldian structure, a method to measure wealth and homogeny. I like the variety in British teeth, the smiles that are all interesting because they're all different. I like watching my friend Jess's crooked tooth flash as she speaks; I grieved when Adam finally had the three teeth in a second row behind the first, like a shark's, removed. But the plastic sheathing my own teeth had started to fail. It'd been there a lot longer than its recommended lifespan. I'd known for years that I had no choice but to go with porcelain at some point. So, one summer, I did.

Let me explain.

*

I distinctly remember, the first time I watched *Singin' in the Rain*, in high school, the sentence that materialized in my mind when Donald O'Connor commanded Debbie Reynolds to sing, and then stood in front of her and lip-synced as she did. *And thus, the birth of dubbing.* What I didn't connect until years later was that, in the film, sound pictures had been in existence mere months before Donald O'Connor's brainwave. In technological terms, the two ideas were twins, one coming only a few minutes after the other.

The word never spoken about Debbie Reynolds's performance behind Donald O'Connor, in a secretive sound booth, in back of the curtain, is *fraudulence.*

It's just for the one picture, the actors say to each other.

In the story, the fraud lasts not even that long. Debbie Reynolds is unmasked as the beautiful voice behind the screeching Jean Hagen and the picture wraps up with truth, love, and song prevailing.

But this is Hollywood, my dears. This is *Hollywood.* The moonlight comes from a gel, and falls on a girl who couldn't dance a step before production began. Her tears could be silicone. Her face dissolves under cold cream, her hair lies on a blank plaster head at night, her little blue shoes are filled with blood.

Here we are, she sings out, Sunset and Camden.

*

When I read *The Lifespan of a Fact* about four years ago, it caught me breathless, like a fish gasping on a wooden deck. It thrilled me, overwhelmed me. I had no idea such debates about truth and nonfiction could take place, because I had no idea that "essayists" had such a touchy relationship with facts. In the book, John D'Agata has written an essay about the suicide of a young man in Las Vegas in the early 2000s, and Jim Fingal fact-checks the essay, which has more problems than a fourth-grader's paper on cold fusion. The two men begin a correspondence that culminates in a debate about the moral responsibility of writing. The book pointed me in a philosophical direction from which I haven't swerved, and toward which my work moves ever closer.

This philosophy depends on a pile of Jenga blocks, though, all of which D'Agata would happily yank out to tumble me all over the carpet. In D'Agata's view, facts are not the point of the essay form, and readers know not to take what is presented to them as firm, verifiable fact. In my mind, fact is fact; facts are closer to truth than fiction; hewing to fact means I hew closer to truth. (That's the point of my whole endeavor, to hew as close to truth as possible.) And if something is labeled nonfiction, no matter what adjective may precede that word, I will assume the writer is telling me the truth: the best adherence possible to the facts.

But fact is not all there is to truth. Not even the greater part of it. No philosopher would let me begin without defining terms, and even though I can't define either word especially well, I know fact is not interchangeable with—perhaps not even precursor to—truth.

In the book, D'Agata argues that, for instance, the actual number of strip clubs in Las Vegas makes no difference to the thrust of his endeavor. He argues that in a sentence that includes the color of a van, "purple" (inaccurate) sounds better than "pink" (accurate), because of the rhythm of the two syllables in "purple." Never mind that this is unmetered prose. He argues that fudging verifiable, scientific facts about geography and speed is not a problem, because he writes "essays", in the etymological, Rousseauian sense, the sense in which an essay is an *attempt*, not a source of fact.

In this sense, D'Agata's license is absolute. But his purpose—ah, that's fuzzier.

*

It's not that I bought the love story between Debbie Reynolds and Gene Kelly, particularly; Cyd Charisse has more chemistry with Kelly during her three-minute wiggle/dance with him than Reynolds has in the rest of the film. But I believed in Kelly's passion, in his perfection, when he sings and dances in the titular rain. I believed his song and dance came from somewhere true. Therein, the power of Hollywood. He's on a backlot, with a bad cold, in wet wool, lip-syncing, dancing a routine that's been arranged down to the millimeter, overhead sprinklers dousing him, and I call that true.

Perhaps what I react to is Kelly's talent spilling like wildflowers across all the prearranged studio trickery. The faker the scene, the truer he seems. Like genuine moments standing out in fiction: Quentin's naked foolishness in *The Sound and the Fury*, or Dorothea sailing headlong into error in *Middlemarch*. Something sublime rises from the painted canvas backdrop and we are shown ourselves, intimately.

Plus, the audience's perception of cinema has nothing to do with fact. It *presents* itself as falsehood. However I believe this movie came to be, whether or not I believe Gene Kelly is actually happy in that wet street, I know that he is not Don Lockwood, dancing because he is in love with Cathy Selden. He is Gene Kelly, dancing for the cameras in a role he plays. These shadows on the wall fool very few in the age of mechanical reproduction.

I can extend this argument to cover the eye of any camera. Even photojournalists are storymakers. Documentaries on true-life incidents are shaped carefully, just as a wooden sculpture is carved from a real tree. But cinema, movies, stories on film, offer themselves humbly (or not) as charming fictions, not charming facts.

Singin' is peak classical Hollywood, a big bounteous musical jammed with talent and money, enough money to pretend anything. Pretend Reynolds can dance as well as Kelly. Pretend the rain is real. Pretend a girl behind a curtain can ever come out and be applauded for her real voice.

*

- *Problem 1*: Patient is allergic to antibiotics.
- *Problem 2*: Patient has chronic strep throat.
- *Problem 3*: It's the mid-1980s.
    - *Solution 1:* Tetracycline or doxycycline.
- *Problem 4*: Giving tetracycline and doxycycline to children under age eight will likely discolor their still-developing teeth.
    - *Problem 4a:* This discoloration isn't consistent, all over the tooth, nor is it necessarily gray like damage or yellow like tobacco staining. It's wavy, and sometimes whitening, so bleaching the teeth isn't a fix. It just makes them look weirder.
- *Problem 5:* Patient is American.
    - *Solution 2:* Composite veneers (bonding) (plastic teeth).
- *Problem 6:* Patient is middle-school-aged, too young to give her nitrous while the enamel of eight of her teeth is methodically sanded off over the course of several hours.
    - *Solution 3:* Just do without it. She'll be awake. Novocain for the pain, nothing for the sound, or the need to lie there patiently while her tooth enamel is removed.
- *Problem 7:* Composite veneers only last 5 years or so.
    - *Solution 4:* Patient will be in her late teens or early twenties by then. She can cope with (pay for) the problem herself.

*

What a thrill to study *The Lifespan of a Fact* in a classroom. The book had changed my life. I couldn't wait to hear what younger minds made of it. The result astounded me: they didn't care about the facts. They sided with art. What difference did it make if D'Agata got every little thing right? He was telling a story.

But it's not the *truth*, I argued, nearly apoplectic. The truth is sacred. It's necessary. It's water in the desert of the real.

Eh, they answered.

I wondered darkly if the internet had caused this malaise. The Hydra internet, for which truth plays acrobat, stretching and leaping and contorting to entertain. The Pandoran internet, brimming with the howls of the damned, splintered and splintering. Everything could be true, so nothing is, so truth sits politely beside the point.

A lifetime of Rule 34 might lead one not to care how many strip clubs there really are in Las Vegas. But it troubled me, anyway, this mass shrug in response to a beautiful quarrel about the heart of my intellectual life. D'Agata and Fingal had impeccably portrayed the problems and the promise of the writer who thinks, deeply, about what he writes, and chooses nevertheless to be dishonest. Because it's his calling to prod his audience, and in his poetics, prodding resembles misleading them.

I can't go along, no matter how well he argues, no matter how dubious I feel about a moral responsibility binding the very profession of writing, creative or otherwise. I can't agree with D'Agata. Not every person likely to handle his work will understand the rich ontological context he draws upon to bend the truth, and that will do harm, to someone, sooner or later. It's harder to write the truth, harder to shape beauty from real facts, but, I mean, that's how the essay is prodding *you*, Mr. D'Agata.

Throughout the entire conversation, a student next to me kept whispering, under her breath, "But there *is* no truth."

*

Debbie Reynolds sits beneath a piano on the soundstage-within-a-soundstage of Monumental Pictures on a Friday night, the lights dim, all quiet except for the vermin rustling in faraway corners. Reynolds cries, volubly, like the girl she is. Fred Astaire, walking by for no logical reason, sees her and stops to offer his handkerchief. This tiny kindness loosens her tongue and she tells him all: Mr. Kelly is so cruel, I don't know how to dance, I feel so alone, I wish I hadn't signed on for this thing, oh, what'll I do, Mr. Astaire, what'll I do. Sob, sniff, hitch.

He looks up. Above the lights, above the three-quarter walls of the sets, the gloom stretches beyond his vision. No stars up there, he thinks, they've all fallen down here. This poor girl. I should leave her to Gene, he thinks, toughen her skin. It's not the last time this life will chew her up.

But she's only 19. She reminds him of Adele in the early days, lithe and strong, fresh as a new pair of white gloves. Come along, he says to her, nudging a little at her elbow, show me what he's got you doing.

My feet hurt, she says, sniffling. Like knives.

They both look at her shoes. I know what that's like, he says. Tell you what. I'll take you to my house and get your feet in an ice bath, and after that maybe we'll dance a little. How's that sound?

If she'd been even three years older, something might have shifted in her eyes, and she might have gone along for a different reason. But instead her face lights up. Me dance—with *you*?

Maybe, he says.

Oh, my, she says, oh, no. I couldn't.

Anyway, let's get you out of here. Your feet will get worse if we don't ice them. He grabs a dolly from the edge of the set, plunks her on it despite her protests (she weighs as much as a wren), and wheels her off to his Bentley.

*

I had ten dental appointments in three months. For three weeks I wore what amounted to a glued-in mouthguard, which chipped and smelled bad and made me lisp and offered scant protection from hot and cold foods. I laid still in a dental chair for many, many hours. For all this I paid $11,000.

When the veneers came back from the lab, where they'd been hand-sculpted, I dropped one in my palm and poked at it. This falsehood, lying here. I had chosen it. In the absence of another option, because the enamel on my real teeth was gone forever, I had chosen it.

They gave me nitrous before they drilled off the plastic teeth. My old veneers had been on for so long they were wearing away, like shale under a breakwater. I asked the dental assistant to take a picture of what was under there. My real teeth are stubby, ground-down, hideous. You can still see the antibiotic staining. You can also see the pink mask over my nose for the nitrous.

After many hours in the chair, after unmeasured time in a pink echoing cloud of NPR jazz that reaffirmed my decision to stay away from drugs, lest I lose my life to them, after talks and jokes aplenty with my dentist, and the unseemly enthusiasm of his receptionist, and the barely shod contempt of his assistant—after all that, I bore new, beautiful, perfectly colored and placed porcelain teeth. No more strange gaps or mismatched length or worrying stains on the edges.

They look like real teeth. But they aren't. Porcelain does not collect plaque, and it feels a half-degree colder against my tongue. They are hard to floss and they sound like glass when tapped with a fingernail and eating almonds feels like eating chalk.

I smile like an American.

*

Debbie Reynolds doesn't sing "Would You?" in *Singin' in the Rain.* A woman named Betty Noyes does. Anyone not dazzled by the film would know this with their ears. Reynolds's voice is high, sunny, tinny. "Would You?" is sung by someone with a natural timbre, a richness, that Reynolds couldn't attain with a hundred years of voice lessons. So even though the movie's plot hinges on dubbing to save a star from humiliation, Betty Noyes hides behind a curtain of her own, singing for Reynolds, unnoticed, uncredited.

There's more. In one scene, Reynolds and Kelly stand in a recording booth, finishing up the dub of *The Dancing Cavalier.* In view upstage is a movie screen. A quick clip of the film plays on it.

```
LINA
Nothing can keep us apart. Our love
will last until the stars turn cold.
```

Moments later, the clip plays again as Reynolds dubs the line.

```
CATHY
Nothing can keep us apart. Our love
will last until the stars turn cold.
```

But that second speaker isn't Debbie Reynolds either. It's Jean Hagen, in her natural voice, not Lina's paint-peeling yowl. The scene depicts Hagen dubbing Reynolds dubbing Hagen.

Deception, layered like tiramisu. *Singin'* is an entertaining hybrid of backstage musical and Hollywood story, and it plays on the real history of Hollywood: poor Clara Bow and her Brooklyn yammer, poor Vilma Bánky and her thick un-American tongue. Certain stars lost their light immediately, in a matter of months, and ended badly, in obscurity or early death. *Singin'*, backstage and frontstage, replicates the problem, and its embarrassing zenith, and its solution (new, young stars with good voices). That is, Cathy is a pawn to the Big Hollywood represented by R.F. Simpson and Monumental Pictures, and Betty is the pawn to the Big Hollywood represented by Arthur Freed and Metro-Goldwyn-Mayer. Someone would have to make a backstage musical about *Singin'* in order to give due justice to Jean Hagen and Betty Noyes.

But no one ever will.

*

A Wikipedia collage:

Dental bonding is a dental procedure in which a dentist applies a tooth-colored resin material (a durable plastic material) and cures it with visible, blue light. This ultimately "bonds" the material to the tooth and improves the overall appearance of teeth. Tooth bonding techniques have various clinical applications, including operative dentistry and preventive dentistry as well as cosmetic and pediatric dentistry, prosthodontics, and orthodontics.

It has been found that after 10 years, 50% of veneers are either displaced, need re-treatment, or are no longer in satisfactory condition.

In a controversial opinion, Dr. Michael Zuk, DDS, comments on the overuse of porcelain veneers by certain cosmetic dentists in "Confessions of a Former Cosmetic Dentist." He suggests that the use of veneers for "instant orthodontics" or simulated straightening of the teeth can be harmful, especially for younger people with healthy teeth.

However, Dr. James W. Dunnavant, DDS, believes the benefits outweigh the small risks when the procedure is performed by a competent dentist. Leading dentists caution that minor superficial damage or normal wear to the teeth is not justification for porcelain or ceramic veneers. This is because the preparation needed to apply a veneer may in some cases destroy 3-30% of the tooth's surface if performed by an inexperienced dentist.

Veneers were invented by California dentist Charles Pincus in 1928 to be used for a film shoot for temporarily changing the appearance of actors' teeth.

*

Even worse, I found out on the internet that *The Lifespan of a Fact* was only *based on* correspondence between D'Agata and Fingal. The conversation about moral responsibility and not spoon-feeding your audience hadn't grown organically out of Fingal's fact-checking duties and D'Agata's artistic propensity toward resisting them. It'd been designed. It'd been shaped. The whole reading experience had been engineered for effect.

Like Hollywood. Engineered. And like *Singin'*, with its tiramisu layers: deception hidden within its depiction of deception. Except that Hollywood's misleading is cheerful, collaborative; awareness exists in all directions that they've made us a happy lie, even if beneath the happiness is the toil and underrecognition of real people, real voices. D'Agata's misleading, it strikes me, is about a position of superiority. In writing *The Lifespan of a Fact,* just as in writing his essay about the death of Levi Presley, D'Agata relied on a sophistication he can't be certain his audience possesses, and he chose to mislead.

I don't know if a writer has a moral responsibility to her audience, but I don't think decent people deliberately mislead others. Twice.

Late in the essay, D'Agata admits that he has bent and deformed the facts in order to draw profound, artistic patterns. Admits it in the essay, but does not admit it to his fact-checker. His fact-checker, like his audience, has to discover this admission on his own. But by then it's too late, and the relationship has destabilized such that the whole thing feels wrong.

Yet my philosophy remains stacked, for now, in its configuration of block upon block. I believe in telling the truth on the page because I have seen D'Agata refuse to believe in it. Only by communicating directly to the reader, by looking you in the face and saying here, this is me, in language, telling you what I am, word by word, without ever misleading you on purpose about what I know, can I write the truth.

Unless I am telling you a fiction, a story about Debbie Reynolds and Fred Astaire that never actually happened. It's based on a probably-true story, but the whole thing about her going to his house? I made that up.

Does such layered fraudulence mean you can't find it true?

*

After the ice bath for her feet, she falls asleep on the sofa, and he hasn't the heart to wake her. (Phyllis is in San Francisco.) He makes coffee and busies himself with next Monday's sides, and then wakes her slightly after midnight.

Oh, she exclaims at once, I'm so sorry.

Do your feet feel better? he asks.

Yes, much, she says. She touches her instep and winces.

Will you show me what's giving you such trouble? he says. I have a dance room with mirrors and a barre if you'd like.

Shouldn't I go home? she says. It's awfully late.

It's never too late to dance, he says.

She smiles.

And so, she dances. She isn't bad, just new. He shows her some shortcuts to solve the problems she's having. He dances with her and she remarks on how light his touch is compared to Mr. Kelly's. He curls his middle two fingers and says nothing. By two she laughs a little when he jokes and her muscles have loosened enough to show the brightness in her movements.

Don't try to hit every step, he tells her. The Foley men will put those in. Just stay with the beat. Don't lose the beat.

I won't, she says. She is sprawled on the floor of his studio, barefoot, kneading her left heel. Thank you, Mr. Astaire.

You're quite welcome, Miss Reynolds, he says, and stoops to give her a little pat on the shoulder. Her skin is warm. Should I call you a cab?

She looks up at him, hesitates for a tiny moment. He meets her gaze steadily, hoping she won't, that she isn't, that she doesn't think. Phyllis being away has nothing to do with her coming here.

That would be very kind, she says.

*

She was right, of course. There *is* no truth. There is fact, falsehood, and the best we can do. That's all. I can't go back to my real teeth. You couldn't make a movie without fraudulence, even if you wanted to; the very stuff of cinema is lies. Beautiful beyond compare, those lies, but inarguable.

We already know that fact and truth bear a wonky, unscientific relationship to each other. We know that we live in a weird era, when opinion can win an argument over fact. We know, from Stephen King, that fiction is the truth inside the lie.

We know that *The Lifespan of a Fact* was presented as a genuine artifact of a specific encounter between two men.

We know that we as readers, unless we are incurably postmodern, rely on what we are presented.

None of these statements are facts.

The biggest problem with *Singin'* is that it's wonderful. It's probably the primary example of its genre (MGM musicals from the classical Hollywood era), and that genre is known for nothing if not its fakery. It's all phony, all cardboard and glitter, ridiculously over the top and unreal. And yet, I'd save *Singin'* from a fire, even if I had to choose between it and my baby book. It is a pure expression of human joy. It's intrinsically fake, unquestionable in its many layers of fraudulence, and yet somewhere between the screen and the eye, a transformation occurs, and the film becomes fine, even true.

But then, this is Hollywood, my dears. This is *Hollywood.*

Don't hold the lead rope that way," Daniela says, in the first hour of the first day at my new job. I am a groom, caring for about 15 horses for a dressage trainer. Daniela wants to be a real estate agent, so she will train me and then be on her way (or, at least, this is the plan).

It's the first correction of many thousands. Weeks later, I will weep, and then close over like a pillbug, from the combined effect of tiny no-not-like-thats lobbed at me. But on this first day I still want to please, and learn, so I watch. "Like this," she says, and reverses her grip. Her smallest fingers close toward the horse's mouth, palm down, while her thumb faces her body. "You have more leverage for when you have to yank."

I wince. She's right that the open-handed way I'd gripped the rope meant I used only my biceps to lead or halt, while her way offers the leverage of triceps, deltoids, and all the muscles of my forearms. But I don't like the sound of "*when* you *have* to yank." I'm used to sedate, kind, unflappable horses, as I've been volunteering at a barn that offers riding lessons to kids with disabilities. The kids are unpredictable, loud, not always in control of their bodies, so the horses have to be trained to react to almost nothing.

This set of qualities is known as "bombproof," prized also for horses in the movie business, because so much loud, bright, sudden activity occurs on a film set.

Within a few days I'll see that the horses at my new job do require me to yank sometimes. That they react to *everything*, and don't heed us out of habit and resignation like the bombproof ones. They are strong, young, dumb, vibrant, obnoxious, splendid horses, and I exhaust myself completely trying to love them.

Loving them is not the point, I learn, sideways, from Daniela and my boss, the dressage trainer. Teaching them to behave exactly as we want them to behave is the point. After the first week, I am hopelessly confused by this mandate.

I find two videos on YouTube that help to define this confusion. One is Charlotte Dujardin, winning the FEI Dressage World Cup on the horse Valegro. The horse moves precisely, carefully, to the theme music for *How to Train Your Dragon*, turning in circles and trotting with high hooves and walking in measured steps along diagonal lines. Dujardin barely appears to move at all. It's a marvel of training, and restraint, and I hate it.

The other video is Monty Roberts, a horse whisperer, teaching a fresh mare to take a saddle and rider within half an hour. He interacts with the horse—which moves like a horse, without any imposition on her behavior—by speaking softly and moving gradually. He teaches her to trust him before he asks anything of her. What he does is what my heart wants to do. But it's not what I've been hired to do.

I must learn new habits to stay safe around these animals, which seem half-wild by the standards of the other stable. The first habit I learn is to reverse my grip on the lead rope. Instead of a clasp, it feels like a fist.

*

Before the second World War there were thousands of mustangs in the Nevada mountains, and [cowboys] had made a living catching them, on horseback, and selling them to wholesalers for children's ponies. But the mustangers had decimated the wild-horse pop-

ulation until there were only isolated packs of fifteen or so roaming the hills in 1956, and it required a small plane and a fatalistic pilot to help round them up. Also, the market had changed. Children's ponies were as forgotten as tree houses, lawn croquet, and family retainers, and the frightened little horses were then being sold for dog food, at six cents a pound.

The Making of The Misfits (1963), James Goode

*

*The Misfits (*1961) seems an unlikely movie when you first hear of it. A single film starring Clark Gable, Marilyn Monroe, and Montgomery Clift, directed by John Huston and written by Arthur Miller? That's a lot of talent to cram into two hours of black-and-white footage shot mostly in Reno, Nevada during a grueling summer and fall. It's a lot of aberration: two very great stars, marked with doom; the aged king of Hollywood; and the sole screenwriting credit of a drama giant. Huston, a reliably fine director and a horrible human being, seems a mundane credit in comparison.

Alas, the film is a bust. Not a spectacular failure, but a confusing one, the kind that leaves you uncertain why the movie you just watched was no good but certain that it sucked. It drifts, without tension or purpose, from sequence to sequence, the characters speaking to each other in Miller's voice, trying and failing to clarify who they are and what they want. The biggest cipher is Roslyn, Miller's steadily worsening portrait of his wife, Monroe, who is described by the men around her as a series of vague fantasies. "She's kind of hard to figure out, you know? One minute she looks kind of dumb and brand-new, like a kid. And the next minute she...she sure *moves*, though, don't she?" Roslyn is less a stable character than a weird, mutating force: sex and mothering, light and pity.

The three men around her—man (Gable), boy (Clift), and jealous would-be husband (Eli Wallach)—could be stand-ins for Miller as his marriage disintegrates. Or they could be a fractured prism of the American male; the screenplay certainly believes it's doing that kind of work, with rhetoric about war and love and death. Seeing Miller's preoccupations under his philosophy is not difficult.

The failure of *The Misfits* doesn't begin and end with Miller's meandering, spiteful screenplay. The central liability playacts as the central asset: those three stars. On his own, Gable or Clift floats a whole film; on her own, Monroe draws every eye. They are so charismatic, these actors, that they soak up all the light the screen can project. Put the three of them together in one scene and the effect is blinding. Even before Clift enters the picture, Gable and Monroe together squeeze out everything else in the frame.

Each actor's presence is so powerful that it's impossible to push them into small, underdeveloped characters lost in Reno. Only dull snips of Gay Langland peek out under Gable—and he's interesting here, in his final film; comfortable and amused, an elder idol. Clift's wounded self shows through his character's ripped shirt and holey hat. Monroe, of course, is Aphrodite in costume as a mortal woman. You can perceive that without reducing her to a sex symbol; her appeal has always been that she is Venus revealed with all kinds of complicated stuff roiling around on her face.

In *The Misfits*, she's blessed with plenty to do as an actor, for once, even if the screenplay doesn't consider giving her the subjectivity to develop her character herself. The surrounding men repeatedly tell Roslyn who she is, or tell us, as if she is a statue. The living actress, though, has as much power and presence as Gable, nearly twice her age. If one or the other had less of what it is that makes us hunger for them, the scenes between them might go somewhere or mean something. As it is, you can barely remember what they talk about to each other. It's just a dizzy impression of two profoundly desirable people doing scenes together.

What I'm observing here is persona muscling out performance. Every great actor fights this battle on the screen or stage. In the case of, say, Jack Nicholson, the persona has mostly won; the part conforms to the actor. Meryl Streep, though, always lets performance win. As an actor, her persona is entirely malleable, except that she's untouchably good in everything.

This struggle is why Huston's own *African Queen* renders disappointment (for me, at least), because Bogart and Hepburn lazily dragged in their personas for the shoot instead of bothering to perform. (Hepburn grew less and less capable of beating back persona as she aged; Bogart only found success as an actor after discovering his.)

Performance never really has a chance in *The Misfits*, because persona is just too big—for each of the three stars, much less all of them together. The studio could not have foreseen this when they cast Gable, Monroe, and Clift. They only saw the asset of these three names attached to one film. But the stars can't mesh into their parts, or work together comfortably. (I'm not talking about interpersonal working together, which seems to have gone fine.) If one of them meant a little less—if Gable wasn't such a king, if Monroe wasn't such a goddess, if Clift hadn't been the crown prince of beautiful suffering—the math might have come out, as it sometimes does when big stars work together. But three legends are too many for the limited capacities of Miller's screenplay.

This isn't the sole reason *The Misfits* fails. The production could not have been more troubled. It ballooned out of control in terms of shooting schedule and costs; Monroe and her demons took the fall for this publicly, while Huston sat at casino tables night after night, gambling tens of thousands of dollars, using the production budget for personal cashflow. Miller kept rewriting the script, continually shrinking Roslyn as his marriage withered. The weather wouldn't cooperate. Everything colluded to distract the film from its wavering purpose.

And, of course, there was one other persona Huston and Miller tried to stuff into a too-small frame, one with more myth and resonance than any living person: the American West.

*

We try to get all the reality we can in this picture, but still you must remember the picture is a convention. It is on a screen with music, and it must be a convention.

John Huston, from *The Making of The Misfits*

*

The mare gazes across the plain. She has come a long way to be here: north across burning deserts and rocky buttes, as far from the men and their leather instruments as she can get. The grazing has been good but water has been more difficult. No one accompanied her except the little foal in her belly. Nearly time for that now.

She smells men very distantly, other predators closer. Coyotes have turned out to be no trouble, disorganized as they are. Mountain lions are scarier, but she can outrun them. Nothing else bothers her nose. What's missing is the smallest whiff of her own kind.

Always there were other horses, always—in stables, in pastures, in camps, in the horrible dark rocking stench of the ship. Other breath to feel and teeth to nip at her hindquarters. Here, no. She doesn't regret leaving—the men had stopped riding her, and kept her tied to the same post day and night, and she knew what that meant. Other vanished herd members, meat on the men's breath. But without a herd of any kind, here on the plain, who will play with her foal?

The mare trots down into a ravine filled with tough shrubs and tall, uncropped grass. A little stream pools here and there in fissures of dried mud. Yes, this will do. Everything she needs for now is here.

She will be alone for a little while, but not for very long.

*

She has ghosts sitting on her chest; ghosts of things she's done, or been done to her; she can't breathe, can't sleep, can't wake, fleeing the hounds of hell.

Finishing the Picture (2004), Arthur Miller

*

My favorite horse, at first, is named Borges—after the writer. He's six, and he's a bit like a golden retriever: curious, bouncy, easily distracted, unfazed by the notion of personal space. He's a large horse with an unusually massive head (it's about as long as my torso), his deep black eyes set against an acorn-colored coat. He's my boss's biggest headache.

"I don't enjoy being this rough with him," she tells me, whapping his chest with the steel bolt-snap on the end of his lead rope, back and forth, like a pimp slap. "He's exceptionally rude, so I have to be exceptionally rough. Otherwise he'll never be safe."

I see her point. Borges has terrible manners: squashing me, barreling through me, knocking me down, nosing into my body while I'm walking him. Like a large dog who thinks he's a small dog, except a thousand pounds more muscular, equipped with fatally hard and quick hooves.

"He's really a sweet horse," Borges's owner tells me one day. Her voice bears a small pleading note. She knows he's dangerous. She doesn't have to plead with me, though; I love him almost as much as she does.

I love him best in the barn for a time because I see the horse in him. He loves people—he gets anxious when left alone, and is happiest on the end of a lead rope. He has no slyness in him at all, no distrust, no guile. He wants to play.

I see him among a herd, in a vast pasture full of calm, beloved animals. I watch him frolic and nip and buck, trotting against the fence, sniffing a patch of clover. It's not his destiny to do this—horses at this stable do not herd—and I feel sorrow for that. He's going to be corrected until he's safe, until he'll behave exactly the way my boss wants him to behave at all times. She'll set aside his horseness. So it must be; that's how it goes in dressage. It's not abuse, but a manner of equestrian interaction. Other styles interact differently.

Weeks go by and Borges improves but slowly. He is okay under saddle, but his ground manners (how he behaves when he's being walked and cared for) are still pretty bad, and it can take ten tries to put his bridle on. He will only accept being groomed in a specific set of cross-ties (the space where we keep horses reasonably still, so we can clean and tack them without them wandering away). He works himself into a frenzy almost every time he's turned out alone into a corral to stretch his legs, and there's just nothing we can do about that. We have to let him cry it out, which looks bad in front of riders and visitors who don't know what a difficult horse he is.

One day I am cleaning Borges's hooves and he kicks me. Via the size and power of this horse, it is a miniature kick; it leaves a bruise about the size of a quarter below my knee. (He could have broken my leg, had he wanted to.) It feels like a test, a little *pop* of defiance to see what I'll do. As yet I have no muscle memory for correcting horses, no knee-jerk instinct to punish them for hurting me. My immediate reaction is to stand up and look at Borges—who is looking at me—as if I am deeply disappointed in him. Disgusted, even. We gaze at each other for a minute, and then he tosses his head.

I tell my boss and she asks why I didn't yank on his nose chain. I have no answer, because I can't explain this lack of muscle memory to her, not right then on the spot. Also, I don't like using the nose chains. Horses are exceedingly sensitive to pressure on their noses. It seems like a choke chain on a dog, a measure I understand as cruel from my dog-loving friends.

The continued hassle of dealing with him causes Borges to lose a little standing in my heart. I want to continue to love him, but he has gone from barreling over me in the cross-ties to biting (not nipping) my hands when I try to pet him. I want to love him for his horseness, but the way I interact with him at the stable does not allow that; how I must treat him, here, pits us against each other. Despite trying, I cannot get him to work *with* me, to see that his comfort depends on cooperation with me. Soon I feel more frustration than affection, and I begin to trust my boss's punishment methods more than my soft hands and voice.

Then, one day, I am grooming his neck and he bites me directly on the left nipple. It is not a hard bite, not painful. Yet something about it feels like a violation.

It would be idiotic to interpret horse behavior as somehow sexual. His aim was extremely true, though. I wonder whether horses understand our reproductive organs as we do, if he was trying in a weird way to nurse. This seems doubtful. I feel strange for the rest of the day.

After this, my affection for Borges dries up completely. He has made steady if slow progress at behaving himself, but he has also repeatedly traded one bad behavior for another: kicking for biting, smooshing people in the cross-ties for turning his back to those who would halter him. It's not that I don't believe he will ever be made to behave himself, but that I lose interest in encouraging him to be better. I do what I'm told with him and offer no excess affection.

*

It's not a business, Phillip. It's an art pretending to be a business.

Finishing the Picture

*

I don't know what other audiences see during the long set piece that closes *The Misfits,* while actors rope wild mustangs from the back of an old pickup, using car tires to slow and anchor the horses before tying them up with thick strong rope—but I am horrified. The production used actual wild horses, which were certainly scared senseless, without a clue of what was happening to them. The insurance risk seems outlandish: famous, expensive actors strapped into the bed of a moving pickup, lassoing (or pretending to lasso) dangerous wild animals? In 120F heat? The whole scenario would be, should be, out of the question, but Huston, in my estimation, did not fuss about safety, of men nor of horse.

All this trouble and danger for a sequence that, all right, yes, may be the purpose of the picture. Yet, as with the rest of the picture's philosophy, Miller's conclusions are murky. If Gay Langford's position is that the West is too civilized now, that "I'm doing the same thing I always did, but it's all changed around," then performing an obsolete activity like roping mustangs is theoretically getting back in touch with the old wildness of the West. But roping the mustangs is literally an act of capturing wildness, of taming and then destroying a symbol of the free open West. Turning it into dog food.

Why is Gay participating in an activity that ruins the wildness he prizes?

What does his struggle against the wild, strong stallion of the little band actually represent? Man vs. nature? Man vs. masculinity? Man vs. wildness, so at least he's taming the West *his* way instead of allowing some other authority to tame it for him? Perhaps each man must individually rope the West, and the trouble is when there are too many men, there isn't enough wildness to go around. However, no logical conclusion exists in a philosophy of every man doing a certain amount of taming, and bowing to no interference about how many men or how they go about it.

Something floats at the edges here about how to live in balance with the environment of the American West—how not to use up its horses, how to enjoy and not destroy—but Miller never quite snags it. Roslyn sees the hollowness of Gay's victory against the stallion even before it's over—she grabs at him, insisting, "Okay, you've won," trying to get him to stop hurting the horse and himself—but it takes Gay more struggle and blood, and a certain *ping* on the internal scale of his mastery, before he sees it too. Then he lets the stallion go. Lets them all go. Lets them gallop back over the hills to wherever they came from.

"It's like trying to rope a dream now," he laments.

What he never understood—what Miller and Huston never understood, either—is that trying to control the West has always been like that. Mastering the West is undoable, like climbing a dune that slips and slides away with every step until no peak is left at all. Like trying to make a masterpiece out of *The Misfits.*

*

I don't like to see the way they grind up women out here.

The Misfits (1961)

*

The mare and her foal have found a band. It's small, just six of them, along with a handful of little burros that hang around at nighttime. The other horses came from men just like the mare did, and they're a motley herd: a grand stallion (once a warhorse, the mare gathered), a skinny yearling shooed away from the men's camp when he didn't gain weight, an even older mare than she who interferes too much with her foal, and an anxious, addled young gelding who spends a lot of time with the burros. They move around the landscape together, cleaning and feeding and playing. Soon the older mare is pregnant, too.

The mare thinks about her former life from time to time—the leather and the loud voices, the chains and ropes (and pets and oats). Her new life is so happy that such memories barely sting.

It's cold at night. The horses find caves and groom the burros in exchange for warmth. After a while they stop nickering to each other as much as they used to, finding it draws less attention from clawed and toothed creatures to swish their tails, flick their eyes, move their feet. They talk without fear this way.

One day, as the mare grazes up and over a rocky knoll, she sees a figure—far off, but impossible to mistake. The bipedal, loose-armed shape of a man. He is alone, wearing very different clothes than the men she'd escaped. In going back to her band, she turns too quickly, and the man spots her and gives chase. She kicks at him, *stay away*, thinking only of her foal, not even remembering completely what men may do to her band if they're found.

The man speaks low in his throat, trying to soothe her, but she kicks out again and, his two little legs no match for hers, loses him on the way into the valley. Back at the caves, she nips and trots around her foal, agitated at the thought of him tied to a post, saddled, whipped into a froth. No. No men will take him away, nor her, either. Never.

*

Listening to stories on The Misfits *set about the avariciousness of the Reno inhabitants, Huston defended the town, himself believing Reno, and the West in general, to be the last stop for the vanishing American innocent. Miller, of course, was saying much the same thing in his screenplay about some of the last free men on the continent.*

The Making of The Misfits

*

After I've worked with horses a little, I'm comfortable with them, but too soft. I can't bring myself to correct them as quickly, sharply, or frequently as my boss does. I want to give them the benefit of the doubt, to assume that they *want* to behave but are feeling anxious or pained or confused.

After I've worked with horses a lot, most of that softness evaporates.

I still love them, and I still try to trust them, attempting kindness before discipline. I do better at understanding how to dominate them without leaning to arrogance, and that's part of it. But also, I get to know them, and that renders my softness obsolete. I won't let Scooter stop to investigate every blade of grass on his way up to the turnout. He's not anxious or curious; he's stalling, and I'm on to him. I won't allow Rizzo to bonk his halter away instead of pushing his nose into it. He knows what I want, and feigns ignorance of the rules for his own amusement. I won't investigate when Clara B kicks at her stall door, because she is fine and all she wants is attention.

That's how my relationship with the horses evolves: I catch on. To their tricks, their quirks, their particular naughtinesses. Love and humor work, but discipline works, too. It feels like I'm armoring a section of my heart that will never again be fully open to the air.

I learn to longe. I break through with difficult and jaded horses. I get to where I feel safe handling almost every horse in the barn, to where I no longer startle as they do but remain calm, collected, a beacon of peace to counteract their fear.

Almost nothing changes with Borges. His ground manners don't improve. His turnouts remain fraught. *I hate this* is what he's telling us, as loudly as a horse can speak. *I'm not cut out for this. Let me go.* It is so far from being my business, let alone my decision, that I keep my trap shut, but I think privately that perhaps he is not trainable. I wish I *could* affect his fate, wish I could swoop in with the money to put him in pasture with a little mare or a friendly burro for the rest of his days.

*

Help.

The Misfits

*

Some of the confusing messages in *The Misfits* hinge on symbols and mythology of the American West passed down from one form of media to another for decades. From stage shows to dime novels to movies to television to reenactors in tourist-trap ghost towns, a huge number of creators across nearly two centuries have invested in a seductive, highly analogistic idea of the American West, one with indelible symbology and dubious tethers to reality. The mythmaking of the Wild West started before the pioneer period was even over—as early as the 1840s, storytellers were inventing a West that may never have existed. P.T. Barnum and Buffalo Bill Cody helped to codify sharpshooters, Native stereotypes, outlaws, saloons, and all the rest. This "imagined West" is far more potent and lasting than the real lives of the men and women who lived and died out there.

Some creators buck against these ideas. Annie Proulx invents new symbology, new values. *Blood Meridian* eviscerates Manifest Destiny and demonstrates what "wild" actually means when applied to men. *The Man Who Shot Liberty Valance* calls attention to Western mythmaking, how hollow it becomes as modernity encroaches. But most do not. Miller does not contradict the imagined West one bit, despite setting his story in contemporary Reno; he understands the West of any era very little, and the complexity of *Brokeback Mountain*, set only two years later, is totally out of his grasp.

As a genre, the Western is almost entirely American. Sergio Leone's work isn't American, but it also is, in the sense that he's using the same symbols and ideas to tell more violent stories in suspiciously Italian and Spanish landscapes. Australian Westerns, meanwhile, reduce to the same salts with a different texture. In the American Western, the beautiful, terrifying landscape and the independent, flawed hero are both inherently of their nation, especially in their improvident scale.

The wild mustang is one of the West's enduring symbols. A free, beautiful creature, catchable and tamable at great personal risk and great potential reward, the mustang sometimes stands in for the American spirit itself. Even Congress thought so, at least as of 1971: "wild free-roaming horses and burros are living symbols of the historic and pioneer spirit of the West." Miller, in *The Misfits*, couldn't quite harness the mustang for his purposes—if he could have, the underlying meaning of Gable with that stallion wouldn't be quite so fuzzy—but he is hardly the only writer to try.

Problem is, the mustang shouldn't stand in for much of anything in the American West, because mustangs aren't native to the American West. No wild horses are. Mustangs are the descendants of conquistadors' horses, brought across the ocean to serve the Spanish and then loosed by their masters from the early 16th century onward. Although Native Americans captured and trained these horses, creating their own horse culture over time, this relationship only began after Europeans had infested the continent. The mustangs roaming the American West today are actually classified as feral animals by the Bureau of Land Management, since they started out domesticated and only became wild later. No indigenous wild horse has existed in the Americas for ten thousand years.

Mustangs aren't American at all.

*

The story deals with a special breed of nonconformist long romanticized by American movies—the cowboy; but here, Mr. Miller passes over the legend of the cowboy for a profound look into his heart—the heart of archaic individualism in the twentieth century—and he has created a quartet of complex and absorbing characters, whose shifting relationships build to a dramatic tension of enormous power. The Misfits *is one of the author's finest statements on the nature of love and human existence.*

Press release accompanying the published screenplay

*

Stories from behind the scenes of *The Misfits* abound. The most detailed record is James Goode's book, *The Making of The Misfits*, which is a journalistic account running from pre-production until shortly after release. Goode was there, he saw the whole thing unfold, as Gable got weaker and Monroe got sicker and Huston gambled and drank enough to kill a lesser force.

So much was complex and hard under the surface of this movie. In Clift's first major scene, he speaks on a pay phone about busting up his face ("My face is fine. It's all healed up. It's just as good as new"), which Clift famously did in 1956, an accident that divided his career in two. Monroe must playact a kind of marriage with Gable, a star she liked to believe was her father when she was a lonely child. Some of her first lines, whispered at herself in a mirror, are the same words she had to say in court when she divorced Joe DiMaggio in 1954. It was the last film for Gable and Monroe, a crewman named Garland Cope, and a prolific 1930s Western actor named Rex Bell. These little knots of pain and coincidence persist across the production.

There are other stories, too: about how advanced the breakdown of Miller and Monroe's union had been before the shoot even started, how much money Huston lost and how he begged for more, how drug-addled Monroe and Clift really were. Survivors of the *Misfits* shoot tell these stories in completely different ways, giving them totally different resonance.

Goode regards Miller as a genius, and Monroe biographer Donald Spoto regards him as an iceberg; his own words, quoted at length by Goode, tell me he was a blowhard. Miller continually reconstructed and reshaped his relationship to and with Monroe across the second half of his long life, often in public. He insisted that his final play, *Finishing the Picture*, was "a fiction," although it mirrors the *Misfits* situation almost precisely. In terms of how it portrays Monroe, it is nearly as bitter and blind as the screenplay he'd written for her four decades earlier.

Compared to these stories and the multifarious ways they're told by different writers, the movie is a small thing, a strange, drifting, toneless two hours. Goode reports Max Youngstein, from United Artists, saying "that somehow or other the conflict and turbulence among the people in the screenplay had evaporated." Alex North, the composer, described the film as "dissociative," adding "The impact doesn't exist when you're looking at it. It stimulates you later to reflect on what you've seen."

I could not make sense of any of this when I began to study *The Misfits.* I couldn't figure out why the film seemed to vanish from my mind after I'd watched it, like a meal that left no taste in my mouth. I couldn't make the stories in Goode's book cohere with Spoto's (briefer) account of the production in his 700-page biography of Monroe. I didn't understand why I loved these actors so much and loved their characters so little; why I would have stammered, under oath, that I had no recollection what Clift even *did* when he was onscreen.

But you can't collect three icons into a small rectangle and expect the rectangle to hold them. *The Misfits* tried to bend a king, a goddess, and a tragic hero to its will. Men have also tried to bend the West, and wild horses, to their will. It can't be done casually, carelessly. They are forces too large to corral with minor tools.

*

You're three dead men!

The Misfits

*

The mare's herd has grown so large that they don't stay together all the time. So large that they break off into smaller bands to forage and look for water.

So large that men have started to pick them off, one by one.

These are the different men. They wear gentler clothes and use quieter tools. Even the horses who remember the early men sometimes trust these different men, sometimes leave the herd without protesting. She occasionally sees them, later, with men on their backs, or tied up and grazing near a fire, or dragging things patiently behind.

The mare feels disquiet about all this. Her foal has grown into a beautiful stallion, and although she has foaled a few more times, she doesn't have any little ones to look after at present. So she should not feel as afraid of the men as she does. Her feeling is not like snakes, fright at an immediate threat, but more like coyotes. The way a straggle of coyotes looks at her and the others—as if they are after more than meat, as if they would devour half the world just to have their way—reminds her of how she feels when a band comes back with fewer members.

She does have a sense of time. The seasons of it. How her

coat grows thick and then sheds, how her feet and teeth must be scraped against rock to wear them down. She can perceive something indistinct but dark about the men, when she combines them with time. Something about her band growing and shrinking, and what the men do with the horses they take away. A relationship. Bonds developing where there was nothing. The feeling she had with the early men, the ones who were nice to her, compared to the feeling she has with the band. How one feels right and the other feels like it's only close to right.

Even though it is safer now, she sometimes misses when there were only six of them. She knew every gesture of every horse in her band. Life felt more like a problem she could solve instead of an experience that happened to her differently every day. A small life is better, she thinks. Not so small as a life tied at the end of a rope, but small enough to see all in one glance.

*

...the making of The Misfits *would be an undiluted horror, not even remotely justified by the final product.*

Marilyn Monroe: The Biography (1993), Donald Spoto

*

And yes, grab up the obvious interpretation that a central symbol of the (white) American West is a feral, mixed-breed animal that isn't from here, even though most people think it is. Look at the lie of that, whether implied or baldfaced. Think about what we exterminated to cross the continent, and the gilded graven images we have set up to distract from our genocide. Consider whether the genre of "Western" should even be, based as it is on a scaffold of carnival fakery and costumes more fun than clothes.

Put all that into what you see in *The Misfits,* in the horses, in the men, in the actors much too big for the little screen.

See what you see. Even if it's wildness, a force that can't be corralled by mere men and that looks inexplicably flat when filmed. Wildness does not perform for cameras or gamblers. It's out there in the West, anyway, undefeated, perhaps unfilmable.

*

Honey, when you smile, it's like the sun comin' up.

The Misfits

*

While Borges was at our barn, he had surgery on his sheath to remove a growth. I learned what it's like to rub ointment on the tender genitals of a very large, ill-mannered horse. This occurred after I had fallen out of love with him. Not long after that, he left us for good.

For various reasons, I never properly heard his owner when she described his injury, so I can't relate it here. He was diagnosed as a foal, and overcame it enough to go into training. But then the injury came back, and that problem, along with his irascibility, led to the difficult choice to retire him. I have thought, but not asked, about how hard it must have been for the owner to choose retirement for such a young, expensive horse. She will have to pay for his care for decades, and she will not get to ride or otherwise enjoy him, except when she visits him on the ranch where he lives.

I have asked if I can visit him too. It is not politeness; I do actually want to visit, to see if he's calmer and more lovable once he doesn't have to stand still in cross-ties anymore. Once he has a little mare in the pasture with him, someone to calm him down and make him feel safe. It's weird, though, because I worked with him for just a few months, and got only experience and bruises in return. Why should I want to visit him?

Because I loved him once.

Just as with people-love, horse-love comes in many different forms. Some horses you grow to love over a long period of time; others you love because you're used to them; still others you fall hard and fast for. I fell for Borges that last way, and fell out of love with him just as quickly and painfully. I wish we had figured out a magic treatment to make him behave *and* make him happy, but that proved out of our reach—certainly mine, with my thimbleful of expertise, and even my boss's, with her lifetime of it.

Now that that's out, I wish I could see him again. I wish I could pet his face and whisper to him that I'm happy things turned out this way, even if it's terrible for his owner. I wish I could love him for his horseness, for his insubordinate, untamable heart, for the part of him that was never going to stand still for anyone.

This Father Film

The flunky from RKO is talking, talking, talking and Louise stopped listening a while back. Budget makes no difference at all. The money would come from somewhere; Ginger & Fred's dancing feet, probably, or Howard and his rapid-fire actors spitting dialogue like Gatling guns. This picture, here, mattered more than any of those, more than money. It was for vaults and history books (and for her), not some Kansas City joker's two bits.

"Yes, yes," she says, cutting off the flunky's stream of talk. "I know. You tell Schaefer that everything's just ducky. I'll guarantee his investment."

"You're not in a position to do that, Miss Brooks," the flunky pleads. A light blazing against his shoulder snaps off.

"*Hey*," Louise bellows. "We are not on lunch."

"Number two overheats easy," the rafters shout back.

"Get that light back on. Let's go, marker up." The set rouses slightly. Louise puts a hand on the flunky's shoulder and extends her neck. That smile. "I must stop wasting Mr. Schaefer's money and get back to work," she says.

The flunky sets his mouth. "Miss Brooks," he says, but she skirts him with three steps, headed for the behemoth camera, before he can speak again.

Losing my touch? she thinks. *He didn't seem dazzled at all.* "Agnes, you ready?" *I didn't use perfume today, and all my makeup's melted off. That must be it.* She fits an eye to the camera. "Smaller aperture," she says. "The snow will wash out Agnes's face."

"Just make it a closeup," says the focus puller.

"*No,*" Louise says for the 40th time at least. "We have to see the *whole* thing. The kid in the background and the adults in the foreground."

"Composite shot," says the DP, halfheartedly. Gregg's on her side, but he's sick to death of the kid's shouting.

"It'll look like shit," says Louise. "Smaller."

"Weirdest damn setup I ever saw," the focus puller mutters.

"I don't want to hear it," says Louise. *Or maybe I'm getting too old. Maybe this is a smarter move than I thought, this gamble of mine.* "Get the kid back in the hat and get her playing. I want two more takes before lunch." Agnes smiles but the male actors groan.

"Have a heart, Louise," says Coulouris, as the kid bounds onto the set.

"I don't have a heart," she says. "There's a flask where my heart should be. C'mon. Everybody ready?"

Nods and shuffling as the actors take their places. The crew goes silent.

"Miss Brooks," the flunky whispers.

"I'm busy," she says. "Speed. Marker. And…action."

*

What is there to say about *Citizen Kane*? The greatest of them all. Ooh. Intimidating. But the story is limited to one life, one man—and it doesn't even stretch across world-shaking events, like, say, *Forrest Gump.* Instead, it's the life of a man who inherits and then expels enormous personal wealth. The film stresses what he does in the world less than what he does with his wives.

All my life I forgot the story of *Citizen Kane* every time I watched it. I remembered the camerawork, and the profound centrality of Kane, as if he was the most important creature who'd ever struggled out of a womb. And I remembered the opening newsreel about Xanadu in pretty good detail. But the story—the progress of one event into the next, cause and effect and everything after—eluded me.

I think I know why. Or, really, I have theories.

Theory One: The story of the movie isn't that well-told. Impossible! This is the greatest of them all! It must be flawless! Well, no. It mustn't. There's a good chance that Welles wrote a mediocre screenplay and dressed it up in filmcraft and glitter glue.

Theory Two: The story doesn't matter. This gives Welles more credit. Maybe he bent more of his attention to filmcraft than to a good screenplay, on purpose. That's reasonable; artists are allowed to set their own priorities.

Theory Three: A life doesn't make a good screenplay. The biopic was not yet a well-established genre with conventions to smooth its way, and wrangling real lives into decent cinema takes a lot more effort than you'd think.

Theory Four: Kane is a Great Man doing Great Man Things, and his journey bored me and left me cold. Maybe I didn't remember the story of *Citizen Kane* because *Citizen Kane* didn't give me a reason to remember its story. Nothing in Kane's life includes space for me as an educated working woman. The affairs of Great Men are not inherently interesting, especially when they're fictional. The audience, whatever its identity, must be offered a foothold to stick around.

There may be truth in all four of these theories, but the fourth one is most interesting to me. It may seem too radical, so let me clarify: the affairs of Great Men are not inherently interesting. Plenty of thinking human beings don't care about Great Men, especially if the foundation of their greatness is inherited wealth, or if they appear to commit no Great Deeds during the time the camera's on them—by which I mean, freeing India with peaceful demonstration, ending the practice of slavery in a former colony via a short speech, or leading an ethnic group to a new homeland despite appalling oppression. Kane sold a lot of newspapers and ran for governor. These are not miracles.

I'm thinking again of *Forrest Gump*, because although it hasn't worn well and doesn't have *Citizen Kane*'s crucial artistry, it at least shows a man accomplishing extraordinary things with little privilege and talents that classify as odd at best. Kane fails a lot, swaggers a lot, and ends his life empty of love. I do not care.

Of course, a key reason I do not care is that I'm female, with no ambition to be Great (or a Man). Cinema used to play toward women more regularly, making subjects of them rather than objects, but across the 1930s, studios tuned the dial gradually toward men as the central characters for audience identification. *Citizen Kane* helped click the knob all the way over. Men were the subjects of films for most of the sound period of classical Hollywood cinema (1930s-early 1960s), and women were meant to identify with (or submit to) those subjects, no matter how little kinship existed between screen and viewer.

I'm too modern, and too feminist, to fall in line when I watch *Citizen Kane*. I don't care about him. I don't want to be him, or fuck him. Since the film is essentially a character study, and he is the center from which all interest radiates, I don't retain the information necessary to remember the plot.

But the plot isn't the point, anyway. So what is?

*

Sitting on my therapist's couch, I explain about the parade. It's a reward I imagine for myself in my wildest dreams, I say. She-Ra is there, and Buzz Aldrin, and Queen Elizabeth, and they're all cheering for me and my accomplishment.

"And what would this parade be for?" Caren asks me.

"My book," I say. "Whatever book makes a hit. Because it's so amazing, and everyone loves it so much, that I actually get thrown a parade."

"Why a parade?"

"Because it's like...the ultimate celebration. They only throw parades for heroes. I want to be that good a writer, that they call me a hero." I cringe, saying this out loud. But there's momentum between us, it's a good session, and I have to tell the truth.

Caren gets that twinkly smile she gets when I've said something endearing. "Would you even enjoy a parade?"

"Well," I say, and think about it.

"Because that seems like...everybody would be looking at you. You don't like everybody looking at you. And all that noise, all those people."

"Yeah," I say. I am remembering wearing a mailbox costume for my high school employer and walking in the Severna Park Parade. It was not the greatest day of my life.

"Not really your scene," Caren nudges.

"No," I say.

"Maybe it's more like an internal parade," says Caren.

"An internal parade," I repeat. Every cell in my body exploding with joy for me. No part of me grumpy and hot and wanting to go home, sniping at the off-key trumpet in the second row or visible dents in the Corvette that totes the beauty queen. Everything inside just plainly happy for me, finding no fault, no fault whatsoever, in what I did.

My entire shoulder girdle relaxes. A channel of warmth rushes through my sternum. "Maybe that's it," I say, cautiously, but my body already knows.

*

LB: I can smoke, right?

PB: Of course.

LB: Let me get this—(rustling)

PB: I've got it. It's on.

LB: You can hear me? Yes, *you* can hear me, I mean—

PB: Yes, all set.

LB: Then...right. Action. (sharp clap) First question.

PB: (chuckle) My first question is why. Why did you make it?

LB: No foreplay, huh?

PB: It's not my style, ma'am.

LB: Louise, *s'il vous plait*. Ma'am isn't *my* style.

PB: Louise.

LB: I made it because I wanted to. Next question.

(pause)

PB: There's no—nothing more to say on that?

(pause)

PB: Louise?

LB: It's itching me. No one's asked like that, so plainly.

PB: At the time, movies weren't art. America didn't have auteurs, not really. *Kane* changed all that.

LB: I'm aware of the history of Hollywood.

PB: And it seems like women's pictures were headed down the tubes. Melodrama looked silly next to the war.

(pause)

PB: So the time was right for—

LB: It all fits so neatly looking back, doesn't it? As if I knew what I was doing. As if I was trying to write my own chapter in the history.

PB: Were you?

LB: Yes, of course I was. I wasn't going to be a disposable

ingenue, or Pabst's muse. I didn't want to end as an aging child selling gloves in a department store. Tossed aside when my beauty was used up. I'm too smart for that.

*

Arrogance is very ugly to me. It makes my skin crawl. I trace this repulsion to my high school, which was rich and white and full of boys in button-down shirts and tasseled loafers. They had skills I never learned (athletic camaraderie, how to do a keg stand), and they walked around as if the world owed them everything, as if the world's payup was inevitable. I despised them then, before I had the words or the life experience to understand why.

Now, I remain suspicious of environments that allow boys like that to flourish. I wonder existentially at the purpose of prestigious schools, of prestige generally. As a quality, I find prestige rarely measures character, or at least not as accurately as it measures endowment.

I go in fear of arrogance. I take compliments with lead weights in my stomach. When I give a reading and people applaud, I make "oh that's not necessary" gestures while my mind hollers at me not to enjoy the experience. People tell me they like something I wrote, and I split cleanly in halves. One half stays and speaks with the complimenter about the work. The other half runs away shrieking at the idea that I deserve to feel good about this compliment, insisting at high volume to beware of feeling warmed by an accomplishment, for fear of turning into an ass. Like poor Bottom in *A Midsummer Night's Dream*.

It's my work and I love it. I never tire of reading my own words. I feel certain about the high quality of much of the work (the parts that make it out into the world). But writing that, just now, made me clench up my jaw, because now people will know I think it. Now people might believe I'm arrogant. What kind of horrible jerk wants a *parade* for being a writer?

*

PB: So it was your intention all along—

LB: Look, I wasn't a fortune-teller. I knew women's pictures were tired, but I didn't know what would happen after I made *Kane*.

PB: You mean what would happen to you?

LB: What would happen in general. To pictures.

PB: And what did happen to pictures? In your words.

LB: I blew up the whole damn thing. I made a permanent picture. I wrote myself into those books forever, for as long as people make pictures, or watch them.

The rest of my career has been all right, the pictures have been what I wanted to make. Going in the history books made possible a lot of things that weren't before, for me. I might've ended up in that department store. Because who would've wanted to see me in front of the camera if I hadn't gone behind it?

But none of that mattered as much to me as *Kane*, as the sheer fact of it. *Kane*'s kept me alive during my life, and it's going to keep me alive after.

PB: Is that why?

(pause)

PB: Why you—

LB: I know what you meant.

(48 seconds pass)

LB: Damn it all. I made *Kane* because I wanted to. Because I'd watched myself burn, watched my films burn, when the studio needed a fire. And because I knew someone was going to tell a story like this. Who'd do it better than me?

PB: Is *Kane* your story?

LB: No. (pause) Not yet. I could always end that way, I suppose. Wealthy and fading in a prison of my own making.

PB: What about earlier? The younger Kane?

LB: There isn't enough sex in the picture for it to be my story.

PB: You played her, though. You wrote the screenplay. You could have chosen—

LB: No one else could have played her. I would have trusted no one else. I wrote the screenplay, I drew the storyboards, I bought the damn chairs for the set. I knew the right way to play her so I played her. That doesn't mean I am her. Or ever was.

PB: If it isn't your story, whose is it?

LB: Oh, my goodness, you know the answer to that. Everyone who's seen the picture knows the answer to that. What a stupid question.

*

If you've played any of the first few *Mass Effect* games, you know that every choice faced by the main character, Shepard, has optional responses ranging between angelic and demonic. That is, Shepard can walk into a given situation oozing empathy and trying to solve a problem agreeably, or he can be a complete aggressive prick to everyone he encounters. It's a pretty cool system, because not only is the player able to make choices that align with (or against) her own moral preferences, but the game's outcomes change based on those choices.

What's hilarious about this mechanic is how little impact his choices have on Shepard's companions. His actions add good or bad points to his karma, a literal tally that changes some aspects of gameplay and mission outcomes. But the people around Shepard tolerate, trust, and fuck him in exactly the same measures, no matter how rude he is to them. He'll say something cutting or boorish to a crewmate, and the crewmate will reply with something generic and benign, instead of stepping back and saying "What the hell, Shep?"

Shepard made me wonder if, all this time, I could've been a jerk instead. In many circumstances it would've been easier. I'm as kind as I ever can be, and I have an intense punitive system constantly chugging inside my head to deflate my ego. But I've seen arrogant people move through the world just as effectively as I do. Or more so, depending on their privilege. Why not me?

Because it's not really my scene, I guess. Even if I could stand to be near myself as a jerk, I wouldn't really enjoy a parade.

*

Film has a grammar. An acceptable arrangement of its parts, an order and structure to its visual components. Generally, the camera should be aimed at whoever is speaking during dialogue scenes, rather than inanimate objects or other actors. Closeups indicate the importance of their main visual element. Shoot over an actor's shoulder to indicate that he is observing what's in the frame. This is stuff you know without knowing you know it. It's teachable, but to most moviegoers it's invisible. Unspoken but plain.

None of these rules sprang into existence overnight. Many filmmakers helped to build the grammar: D.W. Griffith, Cecil B. DeMille, Howard Hawks, George Cukor. Intense European auteurs like Carl Theodor Dreyer and Fritz Lang showed what was possible beyond the standard, but there had to be a standard to hold against the art. As sound film got smoother and less awkwardly edited across the 30s, prestige films emerged, and then peaked in the masterpiece year, 1939.

Citizen Kane was in pre-production that year. In making *Kane*, Welles built on everything that had come before him, visually. He was working well ahead of his time, technologically; he was editing the grammar of cinema itself. Neither creating it nor working within its strictures, but *revising the rules*, showing his American cohort all that was possible within 24 frames per second, even within the terrible spiked gauntlet of the Hays Code. He hammered together the maze that directors would run through for decades, again and again. With one film. *Kane* did all that.

Visually. Content-wise, it set standards in a different way.

It happens that Welles's first film was a thinly disguised biopic of William Randolph Hearst, a Great Man of Our Time (who sold newspapers and ran for President). The content of the film could have been anything, theoretically. Welles's later output varied greatly; as with Kubrick, strains of similarity appear across his oeuvre, but he made films that satisfied his artistic sensibility and curiosity, not films that all did the same thing. Hitchcock could only have made suspense films, but Welles's genius was not bound to genre. Thus, *Kane*'s content is beside the point.

But that is a fallacy. This father film, the whaleboned ancestor of today's common corset, could not have been about anything but a Great Man. It could not have done anything but exclude the nonwhite, nonmale members of its audience. Trace any patriarchal waterline backward and you will locate an enormous male ego standing over the well. Welles, for all that he offers as an artist, could not have made his masterpiece about a Great Woman, or a Great Person of Color. The same ego that created *Kane* without regard for budgets, cinematic standards, technological constraints, or audience patience could only create *Kane* without regard for anyone who didn't look like itself.

It's not incidental. It never was. The towering ego reproduces itself and only itself.

The circumstances *Kane* created, the model of classical Hollywood which shuts women out of the narrative, has persisted too, as unrelentingly as *Kane* has held its place at the top of the list, year after year. In order to prevent this, in order to wedge women in as subjects of their cinematic lives during the classical Hollywood period, only change *Kane*. Position a woman at its center instead. Let its influence permeate across the decades; let its example inspire a thousand others. But how?

Impossible to convince Welles to let anyone else into his mindset. Not a chance. But, perhaps, prod someone else to make *Citizen Kane*. Someone with an ego equally colossal, who cared as little about the institutional studio system, who could not be bossed around or coaxed away from a particular artistic vision. Someone intelligent and charismatic, whose arrogance and popularity both soared beyond the sunrise into an orbit around the moon.

There is only Louise Brooks.

*

Darting back and forth from the camera to the set is a dull and constant irritant, like sand in a shoe. *This better become a pearl*, she thinks. Impossible to explain how and why Louise cast herself, especially when she so poorly matches the woman under this scrim of a role. She's from Kansas, not Toronto; her height and hair color are wrong; her reputation is...what it is, not shy and sweet. But these are helpful red herrings, anyway. Plausible deniability about the true identity she's depicting.

Louise keeps up a constant dialogue with Schaefer in her head, back and forth about her choices. Partly from habit. Partly so that when the flunky comes back (which he does, twice a week), she can rehearse explanations.

No one's going to care about this story, Louise.

It's the perfect American story, George. Every girl wants to take the bus to Hollywood and get discovered.

Not everyone is a girl, Louise.

Half of them are.

Nothing happens in the story, Louise.

It's a character study, George. And people aren't going to remember it for the story. You should see the shot I'm doing up and over the building, into a skylight where Charlotte's second husband is drinking himself to death.

Mary's going to sue us, Louise.

She'll be too embarrassed to sue us! And I've changed it just enough that it could be a dozen other stories, instead. Or fiction. Or me! I came here on a bus and made it big, too, George. I'm a self-made woman just like Charlotte Kane.

It's your first picture, Louise. You need an adviser. I've asked Howard to help.

I don't need anyone's help. Especially not Mr. Screwball. I've made more pictures than he ever will, and better ones, too. What's the difference which side of the camera I was on?

You're spending too much, Louise.

What do you want RKO to be? A second-rate B studio making Westerns by the handful, or a tastemaker? Do you want to be Warners or do you want to be MGM?

I give up, Louise.

She smiles. It's always the last thing he says, no matter how many rounds they go in her mind. "All right," she says aloud. "Don't *breathe* on the light rig. It's perfect." She strides around to the front of the camera. "You ready, Gregg?"

The DP elevates one finger away from the camera.

Louise lifts her arm. "Action." She sweeps a shelf full of books onto the floor. She knocks an epee and a broadsword from their stands in two corners. She swings at a wall filled with framed pictures, and many of them crash and shatter. She wreaks destruction on this husband's study, this second husband whose real name and face she dodges every time they swim into her mind, thinking of nothing except Charlotte's incoherent rage, worrying about nothing except this take, this moment, this truth. The film husband—the fictional husband—is the only husband that matters here. Neither Louise Brooks's second husband, nor Mary Pickford's, will intrude.

Winded, she leans on an edge of his desk, breathing heavily. Then, as if she has never seen it before, she notices an object on the floor. A snow globe. The text on the front is too small to read, and covered by her long fingers, anyway, but she has insisted that someone traipse up to Canada and purchase a snow globe with a brass stamp reading CHRISTMAS IN ONTARIO.

She brings the object in her hand closer to the camera. *Medium shot centering the globe*, she thinks, hoping Gregg can hear her thoughts, believing for a split second that he can. Then, even though she knows it'll be overdubbed later, she says the only word of dialogue in the scene:

"Rosebud."

*

It's an act of arrogance to create art at all. It's a set of choices which prioritize the perspective of the creator, whether that perspective is translated to film or painting or poetry or hybrid, imbricated essays. The creator speaks to the void, saying that her point is worth making, that her voice is worth hearing. That is an act of courage, and of arrogance, if a common one.

I truly have no idea whether a ratio exists between the size of the ego and the greatness of the art, or even the varietal of art. I've met breathtakingly arrogant people doing all kinds of art, at all levels of success. Yet I know from doing it that directing a film, even on a tiny scale, involves projecting all-encompassing certainty, whether you have it or not—and I know that having certainty is easier than faking it. These facts draw people with unusual self-certainty into the profession.

Writing is not like directing, because the people you're ordering around do not have egos of their own. But both professions require remarkable willpower and patience, and each requires an honest accounting of its form's disposability.

Compare early film to theater performances, if you can. The plays' performances aren't recorded; the films are screened for patrons' nickels and then usually burned. The work evanesces into nothing, into ash and memory. Today, films are preserved physically, written about, considered an art form. And yet dozens of films open every year, some portion every week, that are not meant to be remembered. They are meant to add to the studio's bottom line, grant some small fame to their players and some small entertainment to their consumers, and that's it, until they show up in the bargain bin. *Most* movies are like that: disposable.

I love and study cinema and I can't fully accept this, even as I write it. Film must *mean* something, it must endure, it must influence and matter. But the majority of films don't.

It took me longer to learn this about books. Hundreds of books go into print every year that are not important to their presses. A publisher makes a show of caring passionately about its books by tattooing a unique icon on every spine, but the market is crowded with mediocrity and *someone* is releasing those books. Someone is thinking not about posterity, but about the bottom line. These someones know full well that most books are going to fall out of print and be forgotten in ten or twenty years, and that only some minimal percentage of what's left is going to mean something, endure, influence, matter.

The authors, sadly, do not know this. Medium shot of Salieri mourning that no one plays his music at all anymore.

What lasts? What will endure? What cries out for permanence at the moment of its birth?

How do you muster the temerity to make the answer "my work"? How do you set out to make *Citizen Kane*? How do you have the guts for that? Is it ego, or is it something greater? Something beneath or behind ego that knows better than the world?

They never did understand my talent, according to Welles.

If I ever bore you it will be with a knife, according to Brooks.

Ultimately, I do want my parade. I do. I've got my sled, my Rosebud, already. Modesty and meaning are not my challenge. Pull me down Main Street on a float and let me wave to my fans. Celebrate me. I've made art, and it will surely last forever.

Kathy Ireland has an unfortunate voice. It is high and squeaky and entirely unpleasant, like someone's unfunny imitation of a dumb-blonde voice. As a contemporary Letterman appearance proves, she is not faking this voice for the movie role of Wanda Saknussemm in the 1988 Golan-Globus film *Alien from L.A.*

Kathy Ireland's voice makes you think all the worst, most sexist things possible about pretty girls being prettier when they keep their mouths closed. Because you want to hold up your hand in front of her mouth when she talks. You want her not to talk, to preserve her beauty. People probably thought this about Clara Bow.

No one told Kathy Ireland about her voice throughout the casting process, or indeed at any other time. Because she does not control it. She whines and squeals in it with abandon. If she knows her voice is awful, in the film, she's pretending like hell not to.

Also, Kathy Ireland walks with no grace. She galumphs. She swings her arms like a chimpanzee. She does not act in *Alien from L.A.* so much as she galumphs through it, talentlessly, her sex appeal dropping with a thud when she speaks or walks.

And yet, she is long-limbed, tan, tall, ideally proportioned, and clear-eyed, with gorgeous hair and teeth. She is strong-boned but not sturdy; slim but not waiflike. Her body is not the kind you get from workouts, plastic surgery, and careful lighting. It is preternatural. It is a blessing. It's a naturally perfect object, built by genetics or God to be photographed and adored.

Does this seem fair?

*

The ballet happens at least ninety minutes into the opera. The Trojan horse has come and gone in flame; Cassandra has persuaded all the women to stab themselves to death; Aeneas and his men have fled to the sea, as ghostly voices sing him ever onward to Italy. He stops in Carthage for a bit, trips, and falls in love with Dido, who, both times I have seen *Les Troyens*, a five-hour French opera, was sung by Susan Graham.

Anyway, the ballet. Dido and Aeneas and some other characters sit on some pillows and spend 20+ minutes of stage time *watching ballet get performed for them*. And, of course, we as audience are recruited/forced to watch, too.

Ballet is perfectly nice. Berlioz must have gambled that opera audiences and ballet audiences have a fairly large overlap. But it's still an enormous amount of time for opera singers to not sing opera in the middle of an opera. They just watch. And, the first time I saw it, I sat there and wondered how much longer this could really go on. The answer is: a long time. Twenty-five minutes or more.

Let me tell you why *Troyens* is my favorite opera. This is true. I wouldn't lie to you about opera. Are you ready?

*

In 1983, Meryl Streep is pregnant. She is wearing a terrible gold dress. She is glowing and slightly awkward as she comes to the podium.

I knew I'd win, she thinks.

Kevin was so good to work with, she thinks. Such a pro.

Is this what I need? she thinks. Will this do?

The baby kicks.

She gives an enthusiastic, but bland and centerless speech, thanking not-everyone. She looks embarrassed to be there. It's probably the terrible dress.

I love being here, in front of everyone, she thinks. And this year I'm allowed to be fat, because of the baby. I've had to pee since the cinematography category. Half my speech is falling victim to my pregnancy brain. Why can't I do this bigger? No way I'll be up here again.

The baby kicks. Everyone applauds, and the music plays.

Oh, well, that's over. Goodbye, spotlight.

Let me back to my seat now. Let me back to Don. He'll make sure I can get to the ladies' room before I ruin this awful dress.

*

During the ballet, I stopped thinking about the underside. For the first and, as yet, the only time ever. I looked at Susan Graham and Bryan Hymel and I lost track of them as singers doing their jobs, as people who might be hungry or nervous or bored or hot, as talents whose life circumstances impacted how well they were performing for me, who had to audition and learn the material and rehearse and hit their marks and follow the conductor and pace themselves and listen to each other and themselves and hit the notes and give the right amount of breath and feel the emotion and know the melody and follow the conductor and rehearse and pace themselves and go home and eat and sleep and shit and come back the next afternoon to get into costume and do it again. Wigs. Makeup. Sweat. The people breathing in the front row. The man coughing in the back. The lady a few rows down from me getting a peppermint out of a twist of plastic and it is the loudest thing since the Blitz and just what the hell is she thinking anyway to be crinkling plastic during an *opera*.

All I saw was Dido and Aeneas.

The dancers were not workers doing their jobs. They were ancient performers in a Carthaginian court performing for the queen and her consort. I did not care about the dancers' lives, about whether this was a big break for her to be on stage at the Met or how long it took him to perfect that *grand jeté* he just did or whether they had eating disorders or spouses or children or scabby scarred feet.

All I saw was the ballet.

I don't think you understand. I see a movie and I think about the guy holding the boom mike and whether his arms hurt. I read a book and I think about the writer's husband and what he does while she's working. I go to a play and I wonder whether the actors have to sneeze or fart, and whether this is their last shot to make a living out of this acting thing or it's just another night, and whether the sound guy is falling asleep at the switch because his alcoholism is getting out of hand. All the time. Every time. Nothing keeps the curtain pulled against Oz, the Great and Powerful. I am Toto.

And lo, a miracle: for many spellbound minutes, I was lost in the pleasure of Berlioz's romantic French soul and the dancers' beautiful movement and the perfect love story that Dido and Aeneas unfold, eternally, in immortal Latin and immortal opera. Lost. Not to be found in my own head.

That is why.

*

Here is what makes Meryl Streep the most interesting actress of the late 20th century: she disappears without becoming invisible.

Kate Hepburn plays Kate Hepburn; Bogie plays Bogie. They play parts that resemble their personas, or they melt down the parts and mold them, plastic, to suit, like translucent Halloween masks. Their stardom imposes itself on the viewer, because they are Great Stars, too whole to play anything convincingly that is not, at core, themselves.

Meryl Streep does not play Meryl Streep. She plays other women. But you do not forget who she is, watching. *I am watching Meryl Streep*, you think, even while she spins the illusion of a three-dimensional character around you like Shelob's web. She disappears into roles, but she maintains the face and charisma and mysterious essence of Meryl Streep. She is too Great a Star to be invisible, but she is too great a craftsman not to disappear.

*

Kathy Ireland is on the cheap, dim set of Atlantis, the underworld, on the second week of *Alien from L.A.* She is waiting, as actors must. She watches the director argue with a PA and flips through the *Cosmo* she brought with her that morning. It's been read.

The men look at her, like they usually do, but no one talks to her except to boss her around. The women look at her forehead, or her chin, but not at her body or her eyes. Nothing is fun on this set. Nothing is funny, either.

Why have they done this to me, she thinks.

I wish I was at the movies, she thinks. Or at home with Greg.

I'm going to tell my agent about the director touching my boob, she thinks. Even if it was an accident. Which I think it probably was. He wasn't looking at me.

She sighs. Drops the *Cosmo* flat on the ground next to her chair. *Thap.*

Give me a photographer, she thinks. A fan in my face, in my hair. All I have to do is point my hairline at the camera, open my mouth a little. The guy behind the camera calls me "darling" and I get paid, put my clothes on, go home. This here is boring, boring, boring and no one ever calls me "darling".

I'm not an actress, she thinks. I didn't know before. I thought I acted for the photographers. But that's just looking. It's just standing still.

It's the only thing I can do.

And now everyone knows how I walk, and how I sound.

No one sits with her at lunch. She munches a chicken drumstick, tears a wheat roll in half, drinks Tab or Fresca—alone. The women, careful not to look at any other time, watch her eat. They watch her every day. They watch her as if they are themselves starving.

What Is a Body For?

My friend Anna is 47 when she posts, in a private Facebook group, a short video she took of herself dancing in her kitchen. She decided to try and learn the steps from a YouTube clip of Millennium Dance Complex students performing to Missy Elliott's "WTF (Where They From)" Tricia Miranda, who choreographed the number, posted a separate video breaking out each step at half-time.

The video of Anna is about twenty seconds long. She correctly does the moves against the shiny white wall and atrocious lighting of her smallish kitchen, her head cut off above the chin. I watch her lean body do the steps carefully, methodically, moving with a purpose, building a new skill. Then she rushes toward the camera/her phone, offering us a little "aaagh"—something between a groan and a wail—a sound like the holler you make when you greet girlfriends at the airport, but lower in volume, communicating "can you believe I'm doing this?!". End video.

I watched Anna go through these few bars of the "WTF" choreography over and over and over again. I watched the original video from Millennium Dance Complex, then Anna's, then the original, then Anna's. Slowly I realized the most amazing thing about Tricia Miranda's work with "WTF": the dancing is not sexualized. Virtually none of the moves are positioned to show off crotches or bootys or breasts; they are cool, challenging, attractive ways to move a human body to Elliott's bomb beat, but their primary purpose isn't a mating dance. The point is the beat and the skill, not the body. Not the sexualized body.

I wouldn't have put this together without watching Anna's video a dozen times. Something about her body struck me, hooked me. Skill and effect weren't really the hook, nor power, nor grace, nor appeal. It was the *use* she communicated. The way she moved spoke of intentional utility, for *fun*, which belonged only to her. Her body did not exist as a vehicle for any other eye or hand; it was not a receptacle for anyone else's desire or recreation; it was not a ladder for incubation or conquest. She used it for herself, wholly corporeally, wholly for enjoyment, without a whisper of arousal.

The YouTube clip shows people of multiple ages doing the choreography. A young boy does it, and then a group of adolescent girls. Grown men and women do it. White and Black and Asian. All the dancers are badass, but my favorite is a girl of about 13 or 14, who looks as free and fast as a galloping horse. She snaps her limbs deftly, kicks and squats fearlessly. She looks as if no one has ever condescendingly told her what to do with her body.

I want her to stay as she is for the rest of her life. But I know she has her teen years to get through, that more sources than she can yet imagine will tell her what to do with her body, and that dancing might not save her. I know that the world is far darker than the lighting in the "WTF" video. Anna dances in her kitchen, after all, not in public. By the time I start writing this essay, she will have deleted her video, and I will have to write about it from memory.

The evidence that a woman can enjoy her body without performance, without innuendo, shrinks a little smaller.

*

I had no associations for *Last Tango in Paris* when I first saw the film. I was 19, halfway through college, fertile ground for cinema and for youthful mistakes. I saw it because I was a midstream autodidact in late 20th century European cinema, and it's a much-talked-of film from that period. Not for any other reasons.

I only learned later of its reputation. One bit of criticism I read has stuck to my reckoning of the film like a mental Post-It: the correct assertion that Maria Schneider is mostly nude, while Marlon Brando is mostly clothed, as their characters have an intense sexual affair. There exists no pressing internal reason for her to be so often naked and him to be so often clothed. Other paratextual elements stain the film, but that one is evident.

Brando and Schneider come together this way: they are both touring the same empty apartment on Rue Jules Verne. From death, Brando, whose wife has just killed herself. From life, Schneider, whose boyfriend is about to propose. He: middle-aged, soft, sad. She: ridiculously young, finely made, energetic. Their bodies meet explosively—they kiss hard, he pushes her against the wall, rips her underwear away, yanks her knees up around him, clumsily staggeringly awkwardly fucks her. It's a fast, aggressive fuck, but totally consensual. It looks as if they both felt absolute, mutual need, as if they both understood the inevitability of that act against the wall between two windows, and acted at once, without speaking of it.

This moment took my breath away. I hadn't much experience with sex then, and the film showed me sudden, anonymous desire, which I'd never known.

More impactful was what came next. Schneider orgasms, loudly, at about the same time Brando does, I think. By then they have tumbled to the floor without grace. He slumps on his haunches, and she gets out from under him and rolls away, across the floor, her body turning twice over completely—sheepskin coat, hobo purse, soft floppy hat and all. You can see her ass. (Obviously you can, because Brando tore off her underwear.) She curls up, fetal, facing away from what's just happened between the two windows. She breathes a little heavily.

In the next cut, Schneider leaves the apartment building on Rue Jules Verne and crosses the street. The camera follows her casually, at a distance, and the music, ebullient, nullifies any ambient sound from the city. I watch as she jogs across the street, considering what she has just done with her body in the apartment building on Rue Jules Verne. I marvel. I watch her body and marvel. That body so recently in ecstasy now doing such a common activity as *walking*, one booted foot and then the other, transporting her ineffable self from one location in spacetime to another.

This was the true revelation of *Last Tango in Paris* to 19-year-old me: Schneider effortlessly going about her life after a sudden fuck as if nothing had happened. Her body carried the secret of what she had done, but she did not reveal it. I pictured her legs brushing together under her skirt; the absent underwear; the physical residue of what had occurred between the windows, to say nothing of the emotional residue. And off she went to the train station, cool as an autumn evening.

Before this scene entered my life, I believed sex to be a discrete, meticulous ritual. I did not believe that sex assimilated into life the way that, for instance, a haircut might. I thought it was more like a formal dinner appointment, or prom: you prepared, you got properly (un)dressed, you went to the determined location, and you completed the act. Then you undid all that preparation to return to normal life. Sex wasn't a *part* of that normal life, or not a fully integrated part. Instead, it was a special event, exempt from the normal rules. An act apart. A fraught and alien act.

Last Tango shocked me, not with its fresh camerawork or its fully committed performances or its abhorrent butter scene, but with its assumption that sex was just another act among many in a human life. Not too fraught, not too apart. My body could recover from orgasming in order to cross a street in a few moments, and no one would know. I didn't have to systematically prepare and undo myself for the act, but could let sex flow in and between the events of my life like any other recreational activity.

The varied utility of my body, its multipurpose nature, seemed suddenly, miraculously open. What else could I do with it?

*

A List of My Body's Physical Experiences (Incomplete)

Electric Slide
Macarena
Anal sex
Unskilled swimming
Anaphylactic shock
A single 10K jog on a treadmill
Many 5K jogs
Lifting 40-lb boxes for a summer
Hundreds of orgasms
Tubal ligation surgery
Broken nose
Broken wrist
Shaved legs, arms, armpits, toes, fingers
Six weeks of pregnancy
Absolute terror
Genuine rest
Tap-dancing
Assorted lacerations
Third degree sunburn

Gray rape
CT scan
MRI
Kundalini energy
Perpetual callus on right great toe
The touch of hundreds of people (cumulative)
Uncontrollable laughter
Uncontainable song
Comfort
Transcendent lovemaking
Sobbing
Lust

*

Brando isn't physically appealing in this film. He does perform with his body in appealing ways, but I compare him to himself in 1951, in *A Streetcar Named Desire*, when the sight of him makes me suck in a breath. His flesh spills from its outlines: sensuous lips, unnecessary biceps, wide fingers. Almost an optical illusion, how much of him there is to see in every frame. He's bigger than anything else on the screen.

This same body, 23 years older, doesn't deserve the same mythologizing in *Last Tango*. The power of Brando in this film is his grief, his understatement. His body remains mostly irrelevant.

Schneider's body, its generous breasts and sculpted waist, its doll-like face and unblemished rear end, is so relevant it may be the whole point. Much has been written about the misogyny of *Last Tango* and how Schneider suffered on the set, a teenager overrun by two powerful men much older than she. On a rewatch, I found the film's misogyny easily the least interesting thing about it. Nothing is new in forcing a woman to laugh at a man's vulgar jokes, in taking her clothes off while his stay on, in driving her to murder because he won't take no for an answer. I do not minimize or excuse the way they treated her, but I find the thrust of that treatment too depressingly ordinary to bother with analysis.

She uses her body for her own purposes, but few of those purposes escape the male gaze. That's what I didn't see when I was so awed by her zooming from sex to crossing the street. She masturbates once in the early days of the affair, but it's part of a game she plays with Brando, not an action solely for her own fulfillment. She comes attractively and then flirts some more.

We all walk around in these shells for an unpredictable period of consciousness. Seven-year cellular turnover aside, our bodies are our own, continuously, ceaselessly, for as long as we live. The same body. A violation of my body is a violation of my life. A use of my body is a use of my life. The acceptable uses of the body are restricted only by our own shame and will: what we can do, and what we can live with. That possibility space opens wider than I, at 19, could have imagined.

*

For most of my adult life, I couldn't distinguish feeling sexy from looking sexy. Right here I wish I could summarize a study I once read about how young women, when asked what made them feel sexy, talked about lingerie and lipstick, and when asked to give *non-visual* examples of feeling sexy, didn't understand the question. But I don't remember where I read about this study, and when I tried to Google it, I turned up dozens of articles from glossies advising how to be sexy for your man, how to feel sexy when you feel ugly, how to look sexy even if you're old and overweight. So many fluffy, odious results that I knew I'd never find that study, which so neatly demonstrated the end result of absorbing what Google found for me instead.

Nearing 40, I decided that feeling sexy had to do with how comfortably I could slip back and forth between sensual life and regular life. How fully integrated my sensual self could be. Whether, once we'd started having sex, I could make lame jokes to my husband before coming with the momentum of a semi on a 6% grade. I determined that it was about my ability to desire and act on that desire, rather than my ability to *be* desired.

But, for years, it was about being seen. Being visually and visibly desirable. The gazes of others mattered more than what I felt inside the carapace. For instance:

• On a lengthy stay in London, I hooked up several times with a tall, blond British fellow. He worked on cruise ships and smoked a lot of hash. It wasn't an important relationship, but I do remember him convincing me to fuck while pornography played in the background. I didn't like it. To imagine ourselves as the porn performers gave him the power, and made of me an object, a plastic chassis formed of common-denominator fantasies instead of the flesh-and-blood human that I was. Am.

• With my last serious boyfriend before my husband, I did a spontaneous but extensive striptease to Morphine's "Whisper." The boyfriend's eyes became greedy and unfocused, his face slack with amazed desire, as if he couldn't believe anyone was doing this for him. I thought it would make me feel sexy, but it really made me feel nothing. Observed, in a distant, anonymous way—the objective attraction of my body not affiliated with me. It didn't matter if it was me in there, in that body. Not to him nor to me. We banged after and it was fine.

In both of these moments, I should have felt sexy, based on a performance I was giving or paralleling. But those performances weren't real. They were based on external ideas of what sexy looks like, not internal judgment of how sexy feels.

One of the earliest times I felt sexy was in college, at a party with a man I loved passionately. I wore a tiny black satin dress I got from the dry cleaners where I worked in high school, after it had been abandoned on the Lost & Found rack for at least a year. I don't remember the music, but I was in enough of a Mood to writhe around to it, living in my body and how good it felt to be alive, in the world, in love and lust with this man. My writhing came too close to a door hinge, which tore a long gash up the back of my dress—unfixable, unhideable.

It was the only time I ever wore the dress.

*

The week before filming, she goes to the studio library and asks for a handful of his old films: *The Wild One, On the Waterfront, Guys and Dolls*. She wants to understand his performances before she has to work with one of them across from her.

She sits alone in a screening room a few days in a row, watching. He's very emotional, very involved. The mouth, the tilt of the head. He uses his eyes in a way that's conscious of the camera's closeness, the screen's largeness. She's fascinated.

On the last day she watches *A Streetcar Named Desire*. It is mesmerizing. *He* is mesmerizing. His hands, meaty but eloquent; the way he grins from under his eyelashes. The sweat on his neck. She finds Blanche foolish and Stella cowardly, and thinks the actresses do fine work in both parts. But Brando. He leaves her breathless.

The roughneck in the performance doesn't appeal, but the way he uses his body makes her salivate—both at his ability and at the rawness in his gestures. She'd learned that he played this part on stage with the Stella actress, again and again, night after night. This must be why their bodies seem to know each other: Stella plucks at him, he holds her at arm's length. She fixates especially on a scene with a jewelry box, the SNAP as Stella flips it shut, and a dialogue-heavy scene when Brando pats Stella's shoulder in the middle of the word "superintendent." Such familiarity. The pat communicates their relationship better than any larger, more traditional gesture.

After the film ends, she sits back, spent. She knows he is not so young anymore, but she knows also that an actor who can channel performance through his entire body—every sinew, every knuckle—bears charisma beyond the arms and hands of a man in his twenties. Virility will not be the only thing he brings to the set, or the film will not work. Even in *Streetcar* he understood that.

She wonders what he will think of her. What he will ask of her. Whether she can move her body as convincingly as he does.

*

I didn't really watch the Paris Hilton sex tape (*1 Night in Paris*). I watched little bits of it so I knew what people were talking about. I remember it being in night vision, with objects and eyes glittering unexpectedly, and I remember how Paris crawled around the bed, feline and bony. Every move she made seemed exaggeratedly sexy, performatively so, as if her movement only mattered inasmuch as it could be observed and deemed attractive.

My friend Marissa said once that she wished the gendered bullshit culture forces on us could end, or at least pause, so she could understand who the fuck women are when they're not this elaborate performance. Paris Hilton in that sex tape—and maybe across the public exhibit of her life in the 00s?—embodies elaborate performance. *In her body*. The same may be said for Maria Schneider in *Last Tango in Paris*; both women are acting, performing, arguably for the same reasons (to ape enjoyable sexual encounters, to please men). Is one safer or shallower than the other? Or are both women being tricked into believing their performance is autonomy?

I performed so much in my late teens and in my twenties. I came up so short against the standards Paris Hilton exemplified. Sex was the last area of my life I untwined from performance, the final space I had to infuse with authenticity. I had to learn to lose control. To dance for myself.

Bodies are not only for sex, of course. And humans are not so distinct from our animal qualities as we wish we were. I think about our animalism every time my husband precedes me in the bathroom first thing in the morning. The smell of his piss lingers a bit, and I think about territory-marking, and about using the urine of predators in gardens to keep away deer and squirrels. Some evenings, driving home from work, I smell my own scalp, the odor close to my nose after meeting the roof of the car and bouncing back. I conjure up the pheromonal reek of my husband's beard, how I love to bury my nose in it before we sleep.

I think about celebrities who have their sweat glands removed, and regular women who have their pubic hair lasered off. I think about my embarrassment over sweat-stained shirts in high school, and shaving my (perfectly normal) forearms in middle school. I think about a cover photo from *Rolling Stone* that made me ashamed of my knees for years. My *knees*.

All those messages, all the magazines and films and general atmosphere telling me that performativity is the default state of being woman, and that my body never exists for its own use. The moment my black dress tore up the back, humiliating me for daring to move at my own pleasure. Worrying, from the time I was a teenager, that men would find me lewd for bending over to tie my shoes. I fretted about distinguishing my mundane motions from performative ones. I still do.

I'm a mammal. I can't be anything else. Now I know enough to ask: why would I *want* to be anything else?

*

A List of Physical Experiences Performed by Marlon Brando and Maria Schneider in Last Tango in Paris (Incomplete)

Jumping a broom
Tap-dancing
Sprinting
Chasing
Hip twist
Backflip
Pissing in a toilet
Hissing
Growling
Purring
Thrusting
Masturbation
Death
Tango
Shouting
Sobbing
Lust

*

One more scene and she can leave. One more scene, however many takes, and she never has to come back to this set. One more scene and she won't have to see that collapsed Greek face across from her ever again.

Physically, she knew what she was signing up for, taking a part in a sex film. She expected to expose her body to the whole crew as often as the director asked her to. But she didn't foresee the effect of behaving like Jeanne in front of these men for so many hours, for so many days on end. She didn't comprehend how small it would make her feel. It doesn't seem like she's exposing herself anymore, but instead like the self under exposure has nearly evaporated. As if her body has become larger and more meaningful than what it carries around. She curls up inside her own heel, a walnut rattling in an oversized shell.

He stands across from her, swept clean of personality. Nothing in his eyes. Slowly, his face adjusts into lines and crevices of sorrow. He resumes the grieving Paul. His grief is real enough to make her sad, but it's better than the nothing face, which unnerves her.

The director wails and splutters in the background, giving her some kind of direction. She hooks into the sad eyes opposite her instead. The director does the same number of takes whether she's hit it or not, so she has stopped listening. Especially after that day. There's no trust left. She just wants to finish the picture and go home.

He has dipped further and further into his body across the performance, surprising the director repeatedly with new bits of business for the camera. The handstand astonished all of them. As he animates his fingers and feet, expanding into his spacious flesh, she retreats, lets the mannequin of her body perform for her. She watched dailies at first, and then stopped. One shot of her crouching by the window shows her how lovely her back is, long curving lines of spine and trunk down to the arcing horizon of her low jeans, limned in fine golden light. The shot has nothing to do with acting, with skill or gesture. She feels voiceless, disembodied—evacuated from the living object that crouches there.

One more scene and she can leave.

Still locked on his eyes, she does the trick she started practicing after that day. She gathers up everything inside her that's not performance, not tied to the mental energy needed to get through the scene, and drifts away, up and to the left of her body. It all goes on a balloon string. This way, she's distant enough not to have to feel the scene, to notice what parts of her the director handles or the camera prefers. She's gotten better at this. Now it goes faster, and she can drift further. She doesn't really know if her acting suffers, or if there's a visible difference between what she does now, on the balloon string, and what she did earlier in the shoot, when her body still felt like her own.

For now, this is a solution. She can't be present inside the mannequin for even one day more. It will be all right when she has time to get back inside her body, when she doesn't have to see the two of them every day. It will be all right again.

The director calls for quiet.

She drifts.

He gazes at the mannequin, profoundly sorrowing.

Action.

*

Whether or not I want it to be so, I absorbed messages from very early in life about what my body was for and what it could do. I learned that family and doctors could touch and impose on my body however they liked, and it was my parents who granted permission for this, not me. I learned that people (men) are going to infer sexuality from movements of my body regardless of my intent. I learned that giving my body up, giving it away, was more commonly what I could expect to do with it than keeping it for my own uses.

Anna's video looked unfamiliar because I am a woman raised up in the world. She didn't practice the dance to attract anyone, or emphasize her body for someone else's gaze. She practiced it to school her body into performing something new. For her sake, for its own sake. This is a radical act. So much so that I didn't recognize what she was doing or why until I remembered Schneider jogging across the street. The body has a thousand and one uses. For a woman to recall that, lean into it, integrate it, is revolutionary.

Consider the final set piece of *Last Tango in Paris*. Appropriately, it's a tango competition, taking place in a huge, half-deserted café. The shots alternate between Brando and Schneider arguing and artful depictions of the dancers moving around the floor. Even though tango is the sexiest of classical styles, these dancers appear sterile and tepid, moving through the steps with precision but no sizzle. Brando and Schneider clamber onto the dance floor, drunkenly, Brando attempting a bombastic, disruptive gesture against the dance contest and Schneider giving up her body to be toted like a sack of flour.

The music communicates that we're supposed to find this funny, and daring, but it seems obnoxious, drenched in the assumption that Brando will be tolerated anywhere. His vulgarity, and the space his large body takes up, contrasts with the tiny dancers, the refinement of one woman's placed and posed hand against her partner's back. Neither appeals much as a side to take. There's nothing upsettingly conformist about a tango contest. There's nothing magnificent about Brando's grief, about his insistence that everyone accommodate him.

It's the same accommodation he got in *Streetcar*. His body forces everyone to move around it in waves, in wake. Why do no women's bodies demand so much from others?

Why are women's bodies the ones to move?

I wish I had understood, then and on every day since then, how capable the body is. How resilient. I thought it so strange that Schneider held the secret of sex between her legs as she walked through Paris. I didn't realize that every body has secrets. That the adaptability of bodies from one task to another is the biggest secret of all. A body is not just for one thing, compartmentalized from all the others, but a mutable jellyfish of purpose and pleasure. A creature stranger than fiction, and even more boundless.

Champagne Taste

The most curious line of *Mildred Pierce* comes early on, and it's spoken by Mildred herself: *Because I was wrong.* It's her answer to a cop's question about why she divorced her first husband, Bert, whom she has characterized as a kind man. On the surface, her answer refers to the marriage: *I was wrong to divorce Bert.* But since Mildred's entire dramatic story—much of which has little to do with Bert and the divorce, and everything to do with her daughter, Veda—spools out from this answer, it's soon clear that Mildred means she was wrong about something else.

As far as I'm aware, *Mildred Pierce* stands alone among classical Hollywood cinema for the subjectivity of its main female character. Other movies between the Hays Code and the 1960s put female characters at their center, but none of them offers the flavor of those characters' lives as *Mildred Pierce* does. From minute three, when a policeman foils Mildred's suicide attempt by telling her he doesn't want to "take a swim" to save her life, the film depicts people trying to impose themselves on her. Mildred has to concede, because he has the authority, but we the audience sympathize with *her.* We sympathize with her when sleazy Wally chases her around her living room like a particularly mobile octopus. When she boots her shiftless, cheating husband out the door. When three of the main people in her life literally dance while she works.

Almost monolithically, classical Hollywood takes the man's side of things, but in *Mildred Pierce*, the woman is the subject of her story. Men objectify her, but the film does not. It's a nuisance, coping with her beautiful legs and their effect on the men around her. The film considers that, uses it. Rather than excusing objectification as proper and complimentary, it shows objectification as the annoyance it truly is for women.

I belabor this point because of its anomalous nature. Only Douglas Sirk's 1950s melodramas approach *Mildred Pierce*'s subjectivity, but those films still objectify their stars, and Sirk's women want love, sex, happiness—generic, abstract motivations. Mildred wants something grittier. And, as a film scholar pointed out to me once, Mildred is the only woman in a melodrama of the classical period who does not wind up married, dead, or blind.

It's not the plot, but the depth of Mildred's characterization, that compels the audience. She makes bad decisions and chases the wrong goals, and these mistakes ring true. Crawford animates her as well as the screenplay does. It's a full characterization and a full-body performance, its glances and gestures more potent and convincing than its line readings. You can see Mildred thinking, processing. Her moods move across Crawford's body like fevers.

The central subject of *Mildred Pierce* should be obvious, based on the title, but Mildred's relationships—particularly her devotion to her venomous daughter, Veda—power the film. And all of Mildred's relationships subsist on money in one way or another.

I thought I was going to write this essay about Mildred standing alone in a thirty-year sea of objectified women. About how daring it was for Michael Curtiz to model the film after pre-Code women's pictures, back when the moviegoing audience Hollywood wanted to reach was working women. About the persistence of [male] vision.

But I couldn't stop thinking about money. I can never stop

thinking about money.

*

My mother was raised in money. She came from debutante parties, ballet lessons, music rooms with two pianos, a Thalheimer's credit line on her sixteenth birthday, silver sets containing hundreds of pieces. It seems like only some of these signs of wealth made her happy. Nevertheless, she determined to raise me with old-money taste and values, despite my family's middle-class income. She wanted me to go to private schools. She wanted me to like museums more than movie theaters, and to correctly distinguish Haydn and Handel. She wanted me to know which fork to use.

Three objects stand out in my reckoning.

In the late eighties and early nineties, we owned a 1981 gold Mercedes-Benz with a diesel engine and leather seats so benchlike and uncomfortable that I disassociated leather from luxury for a dozen years. I don't know for sure, but I suspect my mother wanted Mercedes ownership without considering the (im)practicality of this most particular Mercedes. It was ugly and tanklike and loud and butt-numbing and I bet it got terrible gas mileage. But it was a Mercedes. Years on, she mentioned offhand that drivers treated her worse when she drove it than when she drove our other car. They'd cut her off more often, would give her nasty looks. Our next car was a red Ford Taurus, the most anonymous possible car to own in 1995.

I remember a rainy day, my mother sitting in the driver's seat of that Mercedes, staring at her lap. "It's ruined," she said. She wore a silk skirt, wet with rain.

And I remember a marble-topped table that sat in our unusable formal living room for my whole damn life. The TV and sofa were in the den, but the living room was where her family's antiques and most of her books resided. The marble-topped table was about the size and height of a coffee table, and it sat in front of a loveseat and chair set as if "coffee table" was the purpose it served, but my mother repeatedly warned me not to set anything on it, ever. The marble top was so heavy, and the antique wooden base so fragile, that any excess weight could overturn it. Thus, it could not act as a table, but could only sit there and look old and expensive.

What use is a lovely antique table if it can't be a table?

What use is a beautiful silk skirt if it can't reasonably be worn?

What use is a status symbol like a Mercedes if it's a terrible car?

I see no sense in any of this, no sense in purchasing an attractive object with the aura of status and significant practical shortcomings. But my mother will always buy the silk skirt, will always chase the Mercedes. These objects represent her refinement, her good taste, her appreciation of what money can buy. And the fissure between that representation and my utter exasperation at these objects' purposelessness is a no-man's-land where we cannot meet, a space containing qualities we are incapable of loving about one another.

I do not care which fork I ought to use. I just want to eat.

*

Laurie, Anna, and I, road-tripping, find ourselves in southern Oregon. We stop for lunch in a small town, and, cruising around, spot an outdoor bar & grill that looks interesting, in a local color kind of way. We draw closer, get a better look at the clientele.

"Oh, no," says Laurie. "Oh, we better not."

"Yeah, no," says Anna. Her voice is tight. "Those guys would run us out of town."

The men seated on the stools around the outdoor bar look to me like good ol' boys. They wear ancient jeans and camouflage hats and encrusted work boots and faded t-shirts with screenprints of fishing gear brands. They have rough red faces and thick hands. I see no red baseball caps, but I spot a Trump sticker or two in the parking lot, which is populated with mud-splattered pickups.

I shrug and drive on, but tension lingers in the car. Anna and Laurie make a couple of high-pitched jokes about whether the men would be able to tell that Laurie is queer and Anna is a protest-attending, ACLU-donating liberal, just from looking, and what would happen if they could. I realize that, far from shrugging, my friends are genuinely afraid of the men on those stools.

It takes me months to disassemble this encounter. I feel baffled and a little amused at my friends' sincere fear reaction to men who looked harmless to me. I realize I'm on another coast than the one where I've mostly encountered men who look like them; I realize I keep different company now than I did then. Later, I realize that as a passing-straight white woman, I present no threat to those men, especially if I pull my sleeves down over my tattoos. I realize that Laurie and Anna have maybe never been in Kentucky, have almost certainly never been in a gas station or a church or a Long John Silver's in Kentucky. I realize that maybe they weren't overreacting, and maybe I wasn't underreacting, but the actual safety of the situation lies somewhere between our separate assessments.

Still later it occurs to me to wonder what kind of person would frighten me the way those good ol' boys frightened my friends. It takes days to figure it out, but I do: clean-cut prep school boys aged 17-21. Boys wearing pastel button-downs and boat shoes. Boys with good teeth and long limbs and blond hair. If I see a group of four or five boys like that coming down the street, I will escape: cross the street, U-turn, duck into a shopfront until they pass. I have done these things, even as a grown-ass woman. Those are the people who read as most dangerous to me, much more so than a coward in an embroidered hat.

I know what boys like that are capable of. I know they've been raised up to be masters of the universe, and I know what training like that does to a boy's moral center.

It's money. Money is dangerous to me. I don't trust money when it's walking toward me on the face of a boy in salmon shorts.

*

A series of flukes has brought me to this hidden neighborhood right here in my janky San Fernando Valley town, which sits on the extreme edge of the city and was once, long ago, the best place to film a Western. A wealthy blind man wants me to help him write a book, a project I think at first is going to be an inspirational autobiography. I drive up to the gatehouse outside the neighborhood and explain that I'm a guest of Philip's. The guard evidently calls Philip's house to confirm, and then lets me in. Already I am profoundly uncomfortable, just from the guard having to call and to check my driver's license instead of reacting with some other, lazier behavior.

I drive in. These are not McMansions; there is nothing Mc about them. Mansions, simply. Serious ones, with wings and servants' entrances and paving-stone driveways and more money than I can imagine flowing in and out of them. I drive among these houses until I arrive at Philip's. His...assistant? housekeeper? shows me into his enormous, woodbound lobby, decorated with specific ideas and objects, the touch of paid experts visible everywhere. I locate Philip's study, in which stand glassed-in bookshelves with no books on them and a flatscreen TV playing Fox News on mute above the fireplace. Everything wood and leather. Masculine. Since Philip is blind (not newly so, but not born so), how much these surroundings matter to him I do not know.

He talks to me for fifteen minutes or so, explains the project, asks me surface questions about myself, wrongly guesses how old I am from the sound of my voice. He tells me elliptically about his decades of life experience and the wisdom he wants to impart in book form, but he does not answer the question that is taking up most of my brain: *how did you get so much money*? Later, he leads me into his music room, which holds a full-size grand piano, built-in studio equipment well beyond my ken but pricey-looking, and two beautifully polished electric guitars. He plays for me the first song of a rock opera he wrote about self-actualization. It is not very good. Bland, like Christian pop without Jesus. Then he gives me a CD of his recorded piano music and sends me on my way.

Leaving his neighborhood, I notice a tidy collection of apartments segregated behind a wall. They are much too small and set too close together to belong to anyone but the help.

*

"Your reason for doing anything is usually Veda," says Monte, Mildred Pierce's second husband, cutting through her attempts at flattery and turning the conversation to bargaining. It's a cold and terrible deal they make, but it gets Mildred what she wants: the old-money legitimacy Monte has, which will draw Veda back like the light on an anglerfish.

Why Mildred wants Veda's love and approval so badly remains an open question. No one in Mildred's life understands it. Veda is a sociopath, a cheat and a liar and a selfish, tedious snob. She lives for money, and she'll do anything to get it, and this is not interpretation, these are lines in the screenplay.

A second open question is whether Veda was spoiled into her rottenness or born that way. Most kids envy their richer friend who has more toys or a nicer house, but Veda never outgrows this envy, and no hardship teaches her to value love or loyalty more than money. Mildred indulges her by introducing her to standard high culture (piano and French lessons), but Veda shows her colors early on when a ruffled dress Mildred buys for her amid many sacrifices isn't good enough. Instead of calling Veda on her ingratitude, Mildred shrinks and sorrows, resolves to give Veda more and better instead of instructing her to value what she has. That resolve drives her through the rest of the film's story. If Mildred had allowed Veda to do without, if the two of them hadn't been locked in an emotionally sadomasochistic pattern, would Veda have grown out of her desire for finery? Or would she have sunk even lower to get what she wanted?

In *Mildred Pierce*, and for Mildred Pierce, money is a trap. The more money she gets, the more she spends it on her bottomless pit of a daughter (and on Monte, who proves equally expensive to maintain). Bert accuses Mildred early on of trying to buy Veda's love, and he's right, but Bert doesn't realize the true danger of Mildred's strategy: Veda *can* be bought, or at least rented. For enough cash, there's no limit to what she'll do. Her grasping leads her to deceive a wealthy, stupid young man into marrying her and then paying her hush money in rapid succession. *At seventeen* she does this. Mildred doesn't see that this quality makes Veda not merely harder to get, but less worthy as a human being. On it goes, a little worn-out circle of grass around the leash made of dollars Veda has Mildred on.

Open question #3—and this is the one that I can't make

sense of in my own life, much less in the film—is why money makes things better. Why it's a solution. Why is a wealthy life a better life? To answer this question I think of abstractions like "safety" and "fulfillment" and "happiness," but I feel none of those things around money. The money in Philip's neighborhood makes me profoundly nervous; the aura of money draped around young men terrifies me. In terms of pure materialism, money helps—more expensive clothes are usually nicer to wear and behold, I'll concede. But there's a ceiling for any luxury. A point when "nicer" draws an asymptote and the distinction matters to no one, except snobs, who chase luxury for its own sake rather than safety or fulfillment or nicer-ness.

For Veda, money and luxury are just *better*, tautologically. For my mother, I think it's wrapped up with safety. The sense that with enough money, someone else will do her crying for her, as Mildred wants to do for her daughter.

*

Despite my mother's best attempts, I did not take to the good life. I quit ballet, piano, and French before I even finished elementary school. I preferred comfortable clothes to good presentation. I laughed too loudly in public. I didn't do anything right on the surface; I wanted auburn-dyed hair and loud music, not tennis lessons and seed pearl necklaces. I couldn't make respectable grades no matter how often I got grounded. Mom wanted me to be a lady, which meant consistently lidding my personality (perhaps for the remainder of my life?), and I would not. I could not.

While I lived it, I envied the girls in my lily-white private high school, who had beautiful hair and even tans and barely-uniform-conforming blouses from Abercrombie & Fitch instead of JC Penney. I wanted their smiles and their smooth legs more badly than I wanted love. I coveted their ease in the world. I did not have it. Instead, I had battered silver Doc Martens, and a motley collection of friends and obsessions and setbacks.

Now, today, I'm grateful to have gotten through high school without that ease, without the money it would have taken to smooth the flyaways in my hair and starch my blouses twice a week. Living like that would have put me under a lid just like the one my mother so badly wanted to clap over me. It was not the same, what she wanted and what they were like—my high school drew mostly new, mid-Atlantic money, not the kind of Old South money my mother came from—but it would have amounted to the same thing: unreasonable conformity, and a cushion between me and labor, between me and common pain. At this distance, I'm glad for the lack of that cushion.

"It's your fault I'm the way I am," Veda sobs, begging Mildred not to turn her in for the murder she has committed. It's a manipulative thing to say, from the mouth of a monster. (The number of times people talking or writing about the film choose this particular word, *monster*, to use about petite, beautiful Veda surprises me, when I start researching.) To this accusation, Mildred can plead innocence, say she didn't know what kind of idyll and emptiness she nudged Veda into by introducing her to finer things. She has no experience with upperclass life.

But my mother knew. She had been surrounded by wealth, and found it comfortable enough, ethically sound enough, to want it for me. This, I will never understand. Could she not see how internally bankrupt the boys at my high school were? Could she not infer how oppressive wealth is for most of those who have it, how many conflicting demands it places on a mind unequipped to make good choices? Had she not reckoned with the accumulating poison of too much comfort over time?

No. She chose that silk skirt. Set up that marble-topped table in home after home. Her definition of a safe world was one in which she could wear the skirt in the rain and it wouldn't matter, because another skirt would appear without sacrifice in the closet.

But someone else's labor would have paid for it. The trap must have its blood.

*

I spent three years working at a law office that specialized in rich people getting divorced. The clinical term for this specialization is "high-income family law." I learned, from this experience, that rich is not at all what it's cracked up to be. Often, our clients' circumstances didn't bring them happiness. Mostly, they had more difficult and complicated lives than I could fully comprehend because of the money they had to shepherd.

I met a lot of wealthy people in that job. I saw inside their finances, their correspondence, their subscriptions, the videos they took of their kids. Most of them were dismal people. They acted entitled to our lawyers' time and patience, and they considered their strangest habits reasonable and sustainable. They invented ridiculous ideas to justify their version of the world—one client memorably claimed his daughter was allergic to hot water. People of all income levels have stupid ideas, of course. But our richer clients were nearly always our more tiresome clients. It went the other way but rarely.

One of our wealthiest was a woman desperately addicted to opioids and alcohol who thought she was hiding her addictions by lying without cease. She told us reasonable lies and outrageous lies, sometimes in the same phone call. She once told us she was injured in a street race on Mulholland, which had culminated in a spectacular wreck, fireballs and everything. (We found no record of this happening anywhere but in *Rebel Without a Cause.*) It proved almost impossible to tackle her situation; a successful attorney-client relationship depends on a reasonably truthful and trustworthy client, and she was not that. We felt sorry for her because she was such a mess. But she was also deceitful and suspicious, and the drugs made her nearly amnesiac, which meant she rarely followed our directions or told us the truth.

And look: the money is what protected her from having to sort her shit out. Almost no possible mistake could drain her account, so she could make mistakes almost endlessly and still pay anyone necessary to bail her out of them. She had so much money that she wasn't responsible for holding down a job or taking care of anyone's lives, including her own. She could just drift, drugged and alone, lost in her own pain.

To be fair, our *very* wealthiest client—her holdings were so extensive that it took more than two years to delineate them in entirety—was totally fine. She dressed in mom jeans and cheap sneakers, and invested most of her energy in her children and grandchildren. I think it was that investment, that purpose, that kept her from being as dead-ended as Madame Mess. If Mme. Fine had cared about maintaining indolence as much as Mme. Mess did, I think she might have been just as awful. But she cared about other people instead.

From all this I learned that wealth does not endow happiness, and that it may instill the opposite of virtue. My husband expressed it neatly: *Can you have a happy life if you hold the values that lead you to have a huge, ostentatious house?* A house like Philip's entails a staff of menial workers, and it demonstrates the desire to visibly express one's wealth without being of use to anyone except oneself. Is such a lifestyle, constructed upon such values, happy? Satisfying? Meaningful? Safe?

Or not?

*

For a few months I work with Philip. He's a terrible listener, and not at all a good writer. His project will never become a book, composed as it is of half-remembered anecdotes and inspirational stories about famous capitalists and iconoclasts. He asks me to verify quotes by Frank Lloyd Wright and Ray Kroc, and I can't; he asks me to edit his work into some kind of publishable shape, and I can't. In the manuscript, he repeats the same personal stories and dogmas again and again. Many of them are bootstrap-themed, and most of them poorly conceal luck and privilege behind hard work and determination.

I try to explain that he didn't hire me as a researcher, nor as a ghostwriter, but basically as a developmental editor. He asks me to research and ghostwrite anyway. I try to say that a book has to have structure and meaning, and probably a narrative, but he seems to think that whatever he can spit out and I can polish will suffice.

This doesn't last long. Mainly because I find myself incapable of doing the work without feeling responsible for it. I do not want to improve Philip's writing. I do not want to contribute to the existence in the world of a half-assed, inadequately planned, repetitively unhelpful book by a rich guy who has tried everything else to stave off boredom and has settled on writing. I do not want to help Philip believe that he has something to say, to publish, that no one else has or could have. Nor do I want to prop up any level of belief that his wisdom is worth spreading around.

Besides, going to his house gives me the willies. Even if he'd been genuinely interested in writing a good (or original) book,

I don't want to drive across his paving stones anymore, or walk on his parquet floors anymore. As usual, I'm in financial trouble, and it gives me heartburn to stand in Philip's ostentatious house, to know that my money problems could be solved with a day's expenses for him, and to cope with him paying me a meager hourly wage to tell him that he cannot publish unsourceable quotes supposedly said by Frank Lloyd Wright.

I make an excuse and drop him via email.

Every time I drove there, I noted that, even though Philip lives less than 10 minutes away from me, I leave the Los Angeles city limits between my home and his. Which means no one in his glitzy neighborhood pays city property taxes. Just the families in two-bedroom ranches a little further down the hill.

Likely not subject to city taxes either are the tidy apartments that lie just beyond the wide rolling streets of Philip's neighborhood. I've seen dwellings like this at the edges of many wealthy neighborhoods: in Malibu, in Calabasas, in the preserve of New England wealth that is Chautauqua, New York.

It would be abominable to compare this kind of housing to slave quarters. That comparison lessens the atrocity of American slavery, and it assumes too much about who actually lives in such apartments. But I will go this far: I will observe that wherever rich people dwell, poorer people dwell nearby, in humbler circumstances. Close enough to be at beck and call, far enough away for school districts and zoning regulations to differ.

In my notes for this essay, I find the sentence "Only decent people are not rich." At a glance this seems untrue, but the syntax of it intrigues me. Unpacking the modal "only," this sentence means that the only people who are decent are people who are not rich. Or that those who are rich are invariably not decent. It does not mean that all poor people are decent, but it doesn't exclude the possibility that richness incurs indecency.

I don't remember what I meant when I wrote it down.

I do know I was considering whether it was immoral to remain a billionaire in the current world environment. I think it might be. A.Q. Smith has considered this question for *Current Affairs*, as have Farhad Manjoo for the *New York Times* and Alexandria Ocasio-Cortez for the nation at large. Mere dribbles of the wealth of Jeff Bezos, or one of the Kochs, could address every untested rape kit in America or fund national arts budgets indefinitely. Keeping that hoard to oneself, more money than one man, one family, could *ever* use, implies that Bezos has no notion of communal human responsibility, the kind we take on when we elect not to live out our days alone in the forest. It's Bezos's money, and there's no practical reason why he should give it up. But there may be a moral reason. It reminds me of that crude idiom, *I wouldn't piss on you to put you out if you were on fire.* The world is on fire and billionaires hold their bladders full.

If you can't stretch far enough to believe me about Bezos, think about Philip. He paid me $17 per hour. I asked for more and he refused. He did not see my time as worthy of the salary I requested, even though others have paid me that much and more. How did he arrive at $17 as a fair figure? Particularly when everything I personally observed about his lifestyle demonstrated that he could afford to pay more? It would have been both fair and kind to pay more, but he refused. Why? What justified that refusal? How did he perceive me, to decide I was worth so little?

I wondered what he paid his assistant. His housekeeper. I wondered how much those apartments next to his neighborhood cost to rent.

*

Mildred's admission that she was wrong, at the start of the film—is it actually about Veda, not Bert? Wrong to love Veda, or wrong to raise her to expect a nice life? Wrong about what wealth is for, what it brings to its owners? Wrong to use money to win over a daughter who could be rented at great cost, but never fully bought?

The film closes on Mildred and Bert leaving the unexpectedly grand police station at dawn, after Mildred has finished her story and Veda has implicated herself. In the second-to-last shot, two stout women appear in the foreground, on their knees, scrubbing the floor with buckets and rags. The floor Mildred's expensive pumps clack on, the floor her fur coat whispers over. The floor she might well have been scrubbing if Veda's greed hadn't pushed and contorted her into a rich businesswoman. I'm amazed all over again to remember that a man, Michael Curtiz, directed this film. Unbelievable that he could understand women well enough to put two of them laboring into this near-final shot.

I look at the IMDB page for *Mildred Pierce*. James M. Cain's novel was adapted by Ranald MacDougall, according to the credits. Four women—Margaret Gruen, Louise Randall Pierson, Catherine Turney, and Margaret Buell Wilder—worked on it without screen credit, as did Albert Maltz, Thames Williamson, and, of all people, William Faulkner. Those women, those contract screenwriters with women's names, might explain why all the women in the film are irritated by Wally's passes at them, why Bert's laziness and criticism grate so badly, why his extramarital paramour Mrs. Biederhof comes through in a crisis and Mildred expresses gratitude instead of having a dumb catfight with her.

Much of this is in the novel, of course. Cain, bless his soul, comprehended and replicated the life of a 1930s housewife far better than a male novelist in his position really had to. At one point, in the book, Wally tells Mildred he doesn't like something she said, and she replies, "I don't care whether you like it or not." This on its own is shocking, proto-feminist, for her not to care what a man thinks of what she has said. It hasn't grown much less shocking in the eighty-odd years between. Tina Fey retold a story just like this in *Bossypants* about Amy Poehler and Jimmy Fallon, almost in the same words, and it was a revelation to me in 2011.

Somewhere between all these creators, *Mildred Pierce* assembles a thesis about how women are especially caged by money, how a need for money causes women suffering. Women's labor is undervalued compared to men's, particularly in the mid-20th century. Women of that era generally had to marry in order to have money. The women on their knees scrubbing the floor, a few feet away from Mildred in her furs, show what the film's thinking.

Despite how women's lives have changed since 1945, money is a cage that has locked me away for decades. Afraid of the money in others' eyes and on their bodies but feeling the tug of my mother's blood toward it. Disdainful of money but desperate to get more of it. At once trying to let go of it as an idea and incapable of holding on to it as a tangible item.

The first time I remember feeling shame about money was in the first grade; the last time was a few minutes ago. I've tried to outmaneuver the contradictory ideas about money I've absorbed from all the influences in my life, from nurture and observation and experience. Tried and failed. *Mildred Pierce* gives me solace, because money makes everyone so unhappy in the film. The worst people value money the most.

But I think about that marble-topped table a lot. I think about how smooth and cool it was. I think about how beautiful my mother must have looked in her silk skirt, and the shimmer of her gold Mercedes. I wonder what I might have been like if I'd kept on with French lessons and worn seed pearls. If I'd lidded all the parts of me I used to write this essay, all the impropriety spilling out of my unruly mind and sloppy body. If that might have worked to make money feel safe to me, instead of dangerous.

Those apartments outside Philip's neighborhood, though. The rape kits. The men and women who have gotten away with everything, including murder, by tossing their cash at the world. I look at all that and I see Veda, the monster, the greedy mouth of champagne taste dressed in silver and magnolia. *It's your fault I'm the way I am,* she said.

Whose fault?

Staying Clean

Wash glass
wash glass
wash knife
wash knife
wash fork
wash fork
wash spoon
wash spoon
wash plate
wash plate
wash bowl
wash bowl
dry spoon
dry spoon
dry fork
dry fork
dry knife
dry knife
put spoon away
put spoon away
put fork away
put fork away
put knife away
put knife away

*

As a housekeeper, I am the pits. I don't have animals, so I can get away with cleaning a lot less than I probably should, but when I do clean, I do an incompetent job. I use up half a roll of paper towels just cleaning the bathroom sink, for instance. I don't know how else to do it without leaving behind puddles dotted with body hair.

From my sofa, where I write this, I can see the collected filth on the grate under my fridge. It looks like haunted-house dust—the kind that drags and drips despite not being liquid.

I scrub my toilets only when people are coming over.

I didn't know for years that baseboards need cleaning.

After I mop, the floor is still dirty.

I do not dust.

Part of the reason for all this is how convinced I am of my own incompetence at cleaning. I never learned to clean right, I presume; if I were doing it right, wouldn't it be easier, and show better results? Why do I use up so many paper towels? Why does mopping take so long? How do I remove the gunk of airborne cooking oil settled on all the surfaces in and around my kitchen without picking up and wiping every single object with Lysol and a sheet of Bounty? *Why can't I get this right?*

Under that frustration lies resentment that I must do these tasks at all. I hate doing things I'm bad at, but I also hate doing the majority of bad jobs traditionally relegated to women (e.g. cleaning toilets, changing diapers). I hate the feeling that I must do the task by default, by order of my genes and social mandate, rather than out of practicality or desire.

If I were better at cleaning, I might bend to its practicality. If I enjoyed it, I would get better at it by virtue of practice. But instead I lie in a morass of grouchy resistance and petulant insecurity, and the filth under the fridge accumulates.

Of course, I could always hire someone to clean my house for me.

*

From "The Laugh of the Medusa," Hélène Cixous

A woman's body, with its thousand and one thresholds of ardor—once, by smashing yokes and censors, she lets it articulate the profusion of meanings that run through it in every direction—will make the old single-grooved mother tongue reverberate with more than one language.

*

The full title is *Jeanne Dielman, 23, quai du Commerce, 1080 Bruxelles*. The film is 201 minutes long: three hours, twenty-one minutes. It came out in 1975, when its director, Chantal Akerman, was just 25. It is in French, but this only occasionally matters, as the dialogue is sparse, particularly compared to its gestures, its edits, its eloquent foley. Jeanne's heels clicking as she moves through her apartment sound like no other pair of shoes in film history.

Jeanne Dielman covers two and a half days. Very little happens in the frame, except that everything happens. The film's fixation on the life of a Belgian homemaker from dawn to dusk, and particularly on domestic chores, prioritizes and comments on feminine spaces and women's work during every second of its two hundred and one minutes. It's a radical act to depict domestic work in such excruciating detail.

How I remember the film ≠ how the film is. The whole thing does not take place in Jeanne's apartment; some sequences take place out in the city, in shops and a café. The long, slow scenes do not monopolize the running time; cuts sometimes quiver with brevity. There is dialogue. Jeanne's son Sylvain does speak, although what he says is both unsettling and obvious, so I may have forgotten his dialogue on purpose.

It's a profound film, I think, an achievement unlikely to be duplicated, unique even in the small canon of slow film for its claustrophobia and its emphasis on the domestic. Forty years later it still startles the viewer to watch Jeanne shine her son's shoes or bread veal cutlets in real time. The slow films I know best have Something to Say, and while I think *Jeanne Dielman* does too, the message is sly and obscure. Even the savviest viewer might get it wrong. Even the most attentive (or stoned) viewer might miss something. Glaciers crack and fall in a moment.

Across the film, objects become remarkably familiar, partly because Jeanne has so few of them. She lives with a frugality intense enough to be incomprehensible in 21st century America. She enfolds the sandwich she eats for lunch in the same piece of tinfoil every day, and then refolds the foil and saves it for tomorrow. She cooks in four pots. She uses two bowls, two plates. She wears the same plaid housedress over her clothes every day, the same thick robe over her nightgown every night. It becomes normal to see these objects, as familiar as if they are the viewer's own. Jeanne does the same tasks again and again—room to room, making the beds and peeling potatoes and washing dishes and repositioning the furniture for day and night use.

Akerman makes this film excruciating, inimitably restricted, so a change in the routine appears that much more startling. It happens at 1:37, almost exactly halfway through. Jeanne neglects to put the lid back on the bowl in which she keeps her cash. And the viewer understands at once that everything is different.

*

Cixous

The little girls and their "ill-mannered" bodies immured, well-preserved, intact unto themselves, in the mirror. Frigidified. But are they ever seething underneath!

*

I had a boyfriend once who was obsessed with making me come. He would tease and touch and fuck me for hours, playing all possible tricks to help me achieve an orgasm with him. I told him over and over that I did not care about achieving an orgasm with him, that I found sex wonderfully pleasurable and I didn't want anything further. He failed, or refused, to heed me.

With hindsight, I see much more going on under this interaction than I understood at the time. John couldn't comprehend enjoyable sex without climax, because the acceptable pattern of sex is the male pattern (see fig. 1), which always involves climax. He did not hear what I truly wanted, which was for him to leave me alone about this. Instead, he chose to believe that imposing his ideas of good sex on me would make me happier.

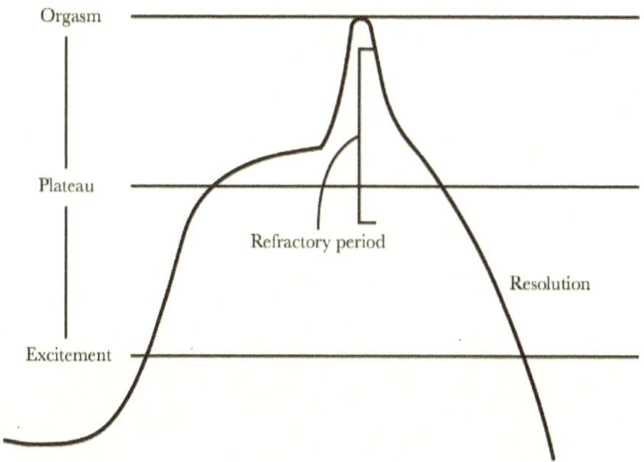

Fig. 1

Worst of all, wanting to make me come was not about me at all. It was about him: about his prowess, his mastery of the sex act. His ability to play my body like an instrument that could pop out approval and validation for him in the form of an orgasm. I had no idea the dynamic between us worked like this at the time. I just knew he wouldn't let it go and I wished he would because I didn't care and I was embarrassed. I thought I might have been defective because I couldn't come, and I knew that the stress of his insistence certainly wasn't getting me closer to coming, and I dearly wished he'd drop the whole thing and we could just bone without any of this theorizing or experimentation.

But I didn't understand that it wasn't about me.

The orgasm thing wasn't the only way John showed me tremendous disrespect, but it's the example that's stuck around in my head the longest, because of what happened on one particular afternoon together.

*

Cixous

Text: my body—shot through with streams of song; I don't mean the overbearing, clutchy "mother" but, rather, what touches you, the equivoice that affects you, fills your breast with an urge to come to language and launches your force; the rhythm that laughs you; the intimate recipient who makes all metaphors possible and desirable; body (body? bodies?), no more describable than god, the soul, or the Other; that part of you that leaves a space between yourself and urges you to inscribe in language your woman's style.

*

What changes for Jeanne halfway through the film that carries her name is an orgasm. It takes place offscreen, but analyses of the film and interviews with Akerman have cemented this point. Jeanne has her first orgasm ever on the second afternoon the film covers. She emerges from her bedroom with mussed hair and makes that mistake with the lid of the bowl. Then she leaves a window open. Then she realizes she's overcooked the potatoes for that night's dinner. Her movements become chaotic, uncertain. She can no longer make sense of her life, contained as it always has been in the small spaces of this film, with no possible outreach into bliss.

It's tightly composed, *Jeanne Dielman*, with direct angles and methodical shot lengths. Enough time to see Jeanne come into the frame, perform an action, and leave the frame, on almost every occasion. Only enough space in the frame for Jeanne and her immediate surroundings. Like television: meant for a small space and a short depth of focus. Similarly, the small spaces of Jeanne's life leave room for nothing but responsibilities.

The only moments she betrays a chore-free identity revolve around coffee. On the second morning, she drinks a cup just off the stove, crossing her feet cutely. The coffee brings her real pleasure (*plaisir*, not *jouissance*). In the afternoon, she puts on lipstick and goes to a café, sitting quietly, gazing out the window, drinking her coffee in short gulps. At nearly all other times, she cleans, cooks, cares for, arranges, services.

Jeanne does not have a job, except that she has sex with men for money. Three of them, one on each of the film's three days. The men are completely undistinguished, in a range of middle age, neither repellent nor attractive. It's unknown whether she has a client for every day of the week, or just these three. The film offers no information about how Jeanne got into this line of work, where her clients come from, whether she finds the work demeaning. It depicts the tasks she does in enormous detail, start to finish, except this one chore. When the first two clients visit, the bedroom door closes and does not open until the winter light in the hallway has changed, from midafternoon to dusk. An hour, perhaps. As long as it takes to cook the potatoes for dinner.

In *Pleasantville* (1998), Joan Allen's first-ever orgasm causes the tree outside her house to explode into orange flame. But that is an orgasm she gives herself, in the bath. Jeanne's orgasm comes from her second client. Since the door remains closed, we cannot know what was different for her, what either of them did or didn't do to affect this change. It's only Jeanne's messy hair, and the remaining events of the film, that hint at what happened in any way.

And misinterpreting this subtext is fairly easy to do.

*

Cixous	Who, feeling a funny desire stirring inside her (to sing, to write, to dare to speak, in short, to bring out something new), hasn't thought she was sick?

*

The specific acts John performed on me that day are no longer in my memory, but I know that I'd asked him to drop the issue for the day so we could do something else—eat a meal, probably—and he insisted that he just wanted to try this one thing. I lay back and thought of nothing. What he did gave me physical pleasure and emotional frustration. The pleasure was a kind of torment, because it built without ebbing or peaking, because I wanted it to stop and it would not, because I was not having any fun.

Then my body began to laugh. I put it that way because that was my experience: not that something made me laugh, but that my body spontaneously erupted into laughter. Like a geyser at a hot spring: the result of pressure over time, explosively, messily releasing. My body laughed, and John moved away from me and watched me dissolve into loud, diaphragm-shaking, uncontrollable laughter without explanation. In a blink, the laughter transformed into tears.

John looked at me, at a loss. I had become an incomprehensible machine. He did not know why my body did what it did. Neither did I.

Sometimes I read stories about child sexual abuse wherein the child urinates or vomits in a kind of semi-autonomic attempt to stop what's happening to them. Their bodies are imposed upon, and the bodies rebel. The response isn't guaranteed, nor is it necessarily something the child has consciously thought out as a defense. I abhor that bodies are forced into such corners, of course, but it fascinates me that these bodies find unexpected defenses. That those defenses are neither force nor wit, but something else.

John was not abusing me, but he was doing something to my body that my body and I did not want him to do. My body's solution was laughter. I wonder if she would have gone to more extreme measures if John hadn't been so weirded out by her response.

*

Cixous

And I, too, said nothing, showed nothing;
I didn't open my mouth, I didn't repaint
my half of the world. I was ashamed.

*

In *The Money Pit* (1986), Shelley Long folds a couple of button-down shirts while packing clothes. She aligns the shoulders and cuffs and then folds the cuffs diagonally toward the belly of the shirt, and then folds the whole thing over, collar to tail (see fig. 2), before dropping it into a suitcase.

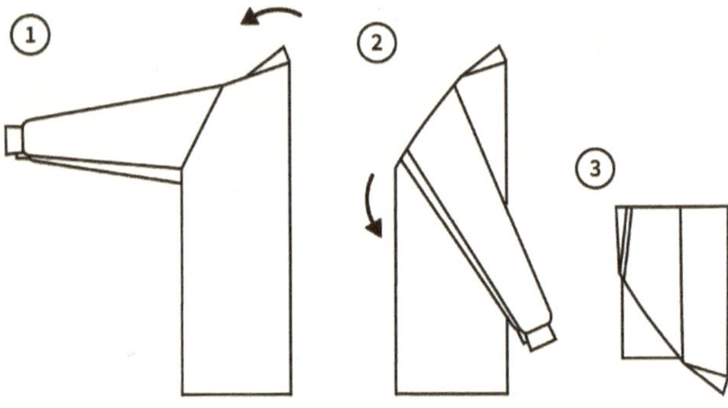

Fig. 2

I did not learn to fold shirts this way, and when I saw her do it in the movie I was surprised. Subsequently I tried folding shirts that way, but it seemed messy and unintuitive, failing to match the shirt's natural lines. I fold them by crossing the arms behind the back and folding the tail toward the collar with the arms inside (see fig. 3). It makes a rectangle instead of a…trapezoid, I guess.

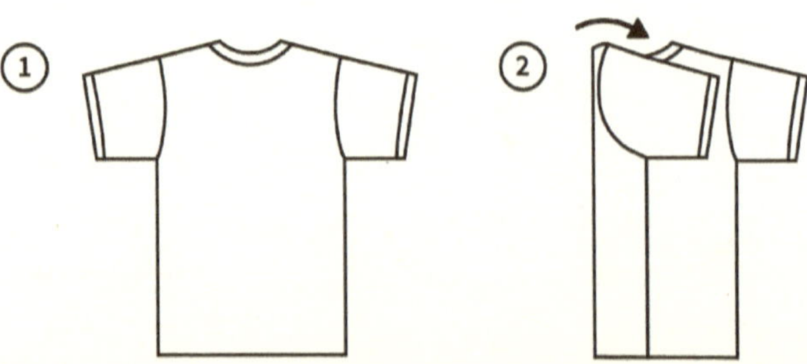

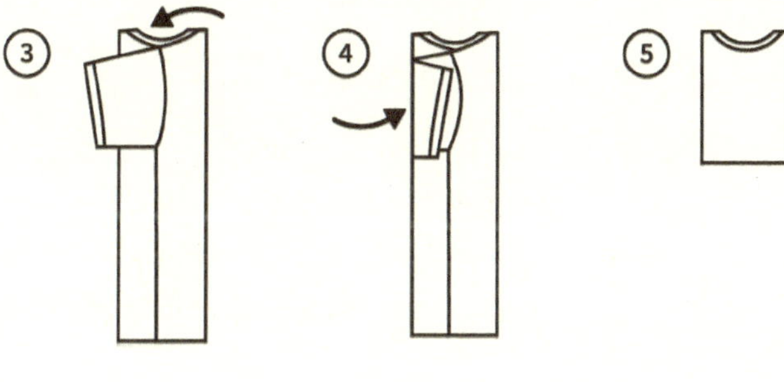

Fig. 3

Every time an actress folds a shirt I watch. More often than not, they fold it like Shelley Long, with the sleeves diagonal to the midline. Delphine Seyrig folds shirts this way, too, in *Jeanne Dielman.*

It occurs to me in describing this action that Long's method doesn't require a surface to fold the shirt, while mine needs a spot to lay the shirt out. Maybe that's why the first method is more common on camera. But I've always assumed it's a different-strokes thing—that the actress's mother taught her to fold shirts that way, so even when playing a different woman in front of a camera, she folds them that way.

I didn't believe this action on film could matter so much that a director would specify how he wanted the shirt folded. It was too small a gesture, too irrelevant to the plot of the average film, and anyway what do male directors know about folding shirts?

The documentaries about *Jeanne Dielman* reveal that Akerman and Seyrig plotted every movement in every scene with exhausting precision. Seyrig had to learn how to do many of the domestic tasks, as she had chosen a way of life (being a glamorous French actress) that did not require her to shine shoes or brew coffee. But surely she had a particular habit or preference for folding shirts. Surely she and Akerman discussed it and settled on the diagonal-sleeve method for a reason.

*

Delphine Seyrig, on the ordinary domestic actions depicted in the film

We accept that these things are done by certain people—predominantly women—when it shouldn't just be accepted—How to explain?—Women who do these things every day know what I mean, because they believe that everyone thinks it's nat-ural for them to do them, when it's not natural at all.

*

straighten sheet
straighten sheet
tuck sheet
tuck sheet
tuck sheet
tuck sheet
straighten blanket
straighten blanket
fold nightgown
replace pillow
unfold coverlet
straighten coverlet
straighten coverlet
straighten coverlet

*

Cixous

When the "repressed" of their culture and their society returns, it's an explosive, *utterly* destructive, staggering return, with a force never yet unleashed and equal to the most forbidding of suppressions. For when the Phallic period comes to an end, women will have been either annihilated or borne up to the highest and most violent incandescence. Muffled throughout their history, they have lived in dreams, in bodies (though muted), in silences, in aphonic revolts.

*

In order to get our security deposit back on an apartment we'd rented for a year, I decided to hire a maid service to clean the place. I felt helpless at the task of making the apartment clean enough for a landlord's inspection. The pleasant but businesslike woman I led around our place, to explain what needed to be done, was short, sturdy, and Latina.

When I showed her the tub where we most often showered, she winced at the dingy buildup of soap and dead skin cells in a semicircle around the floor. She had not reacted to any other aspect of my housekeeping, even though my brain shouted at me all through the tour about how ashamed of myself I should be, that I didn't dust and couldn't mop and hadn't cleaned the baseboards. That one visible wince, with its small accompanying noise of the hassle my bathtub represented, washed me with such shame that I wanted to lie down in the dirty tub and pull the curtain, so she could no longer see me.

It's disproportionate, the shame I feel about my inadequacies as a housekeeper. I know I'm not the only person who disdains cleaning and/or is bad at it, and I know I'm good at other things. I'm even good at other *domestic* things. But it seems like I've failed at something significant by failing to clean. Whether or not it's hooked in to my gender I haven't decided.

The situation with the visible wince isn't the only time I've hired cleaners. From time to time, in every home I've lived in, I get fed up and call in the pros. I stay out of their way; I tip them well; I compliment them and say I'll hire them again for a regular gig. But I don't. Outsourcing the job of cleaning up my mess feels like an abdication of my responsibility as a human being. Like I'm passing necessary labor down the chain until someone, down there, has to do twice as much as I have to do: their own labor and someone else's too. It feels like I'm exploiting someone for the sake of my own comfort, which is a morally intolerable idea.

This might seem hysterical. Service jobs are not new; people have paid other people to clean up after them for millennia. Yet that simply implies, to me, millennia of exploitation in exchange for comfort. How likely is it that every person employed to clean actually enjoys cleaning? That they are paid a fair wage for this often unpleasant task? That this wasn't the only job they could get, that they are content with such work?

Do exploitation and employment look so similar?

Friends have argued that it's better to offer payment for a cleaning job to a person who's miserable doing it than no payment for any job. But I can't participate in the perpetuation of that job without my conscience shrieking at me, good intentions or no. I worry too much about what they're thinking, what they *could* be thinking if they weren't concentrating on cleaning up my mess, what they could be doing with that mental energy.

So I sit in my dirty house, feeling bad. Literally or morally,

I don't know how to stay clean.

*

Cixous	Women's imaginary is inexhaustible... their stream of phantasms is incredible.

*

On the third day, everything goes wrong. The shops where Jeanne does her errands aren't open when she visits them. Someone sits at her usual table in the café. She traipses all over Brussels looking for a button for her son's coat. When she comes home, she finds herself with time she can't fill; for three entire minutes, she sits in a chair, breathing, as we watch.

Then her third client arrives. The film is nearly over when it shows what's been going on in the bedroom this entire time. It's a sex scene, surprising only inasmuch as we ask ourselves what we expected to see if not this. A man in a white undershirt lies atop Jeanne, breathing thickly. Her eyes dart around, her face expressing something between discomfort and panic. The man barely moves, and then Jeanne starts moving. She goes through some kind of paroxysm, burying her face in the greenish coverlet, pushing at the man's arms and shoulders ineffectually, writhing like she wants to escape, emitting small sounds. A few moments later, this episode ends, Jeanne's arm half-slung over the man's neck, both of them breathing. Cut to Jeanne at her dressing table, buttoning her blouse, as the man sits, then lounges on the bed behind her.

I saw *Jeanne Dielman* in adult life, after I'd read a hundred terrible stories of men doing whatever they wanted to women, after I'd been coerced into sex I didn't want to have, after I'd learned to focus and modulate my own pleasure, after I tried most of what I wanted to and learned to say no to what I didn't. And this scene looked to me like rape. Jeanne wriggles in misery. She turns her face away from the heavy man pressing down on her. She shoves at him with her hands. She looks to me like she's trying to stop or block out what's happening to her body. Her resistance is obvious. To me.

I have discovered that this interpretation is wrong. Film scholars read the scene as an orgasm. Akerman explains the scene as an orgasm. Delphine Seyrig played the scene as an orgasm. I watched the film again, and rewound and watched the scene twice more. It still reads to me as rape.

The other way to interpret the second client's impact on Jeanne, what causes her routine to go so awry, is as trauma. She cannot get her life on track after the second client's visit because he has harmed her, has done something to her without her consent. She is plainly disturbed in the scenes that follow, and her disturbance could be grounded in injury.

But Akerman's point is that the orgasm *is* disturbing to Jeanne. It's a catastrophic force, because her life has almost no pleasure in it. (Just that one cup of coffee, when she crossed her ankles and drank deeply.) For a repressed European widow who survived the second World War, life must fit into the structures of routine and service. Personal pleasure is unthinkable, as destructive as a tree on fire.

What I can't pin down: why the scene with the third client is acted and filmed as it is. Jeanne could be resisting the very idea of personal pleasure, not wanting her life to collapse into chaos now that she knows about this thing her body can do. But this is not a world where a woman lying beneath a man who is paying her for sex can squirm and resist without rape in the subtext. Belgium in 1975 was not that world, either.

It continues to annoy me that I can't read this scene in the way it was meant. I still see rape in it, no matter how many sources tell me it's not.

Do rape and orgasm look so similar?

*

Cixous You only have to look at the Medusa straight on to see her. And she's not deadly. She's beautiful and she's laughing.

*

Jeanne Dielman narrows the frame of film to women's work. Jeanne cooks, cleans, shops, and fucks men for money. Akerman implies that all of these are joyless chores, and that the one is no more salacious than the rest. Speculating about why Jeanne has sanded down her life until it fits into tiny, organized polygons of activity—that is for scholars, not dabblers like me. I think it's about World War II, scarcity and security, but I'm not nearly as interested in that as I am in the third client. That orgasm. The human body in ecstasy is difficult to portray with both beauty and accuracy; usually an actor must pick one or the other. That I misread Seyrig may be my fault, not hers.

Jeanne's pleasure proves disastrous to her woman's work. Whether I misinterpreted the scene or not, Jeanne's orgasm *is* a trauma: a moment in which her body flutters out of her tight control. My body, unprepared for what it was being urged to do, laughed. Jeanne's does something else.

Her mind remains unknowable.

Since the film has so little dialogue, and focuses on repetitive action, its great, continuous mystery is what Jeanne is thinking during her day. The notion that she could be thinking more sophisticated thoughts than the required processing of what's in front of her—the question of what other tasks she could set her mind to—the stupefying realization that these same domestic tasks have filled her life for decades, with no room left for ideas of her own—

and I cannot bear either to clean my own apartment, or to pay another thinking human being to do it for me.

*

peel potato
peel potato
peel potato
peel potato
peel potato
peel potato
peel potato
peel potato
rinse potato
peel potato
peel potato
peel potato
peel potato
peel potato
peel potato
peel potato
peel potato
rinse potato
peel potato
peel potato
peel potato
peel potato

peel potato
peel potato
peel potato
peel potato
rinse potato
peel potato
peel potato
peel potato
peel potato
peel potato
peel potato
peel potato
peel potato
rinse potato

Notes

This isn't a scholarly book, so it doesn't include a scholarly bibliography. I'm not going to list every film or book I mentioned (nor, for example, the dozen or so books I've read about Marilyn Monroe). But some of these books are genuinely sources, not just influences, so it wouldn't be right not to give them their due.

Also, when not specifically notated, the stories I tell about actors and other creative figures are inventions of my imagination. I intend for no one to take them as fact, nor to believe I am embellishing true stories. For instance, if Robert Duvall is on record about how he approached his big monologue in *Apocalypse Now,* I am unaware of what he said; I made up thoughts and feelings for him and assigned them to the persona given his name. The same goes for every public figure in this book—again, unless otherwise noted.

Butler, Carolyn Kleiner. "Coming Home." *Smithsonian Magazine* (online), January 2005.

Brooks, Louise. *Lulu in Hollywood.* Minneapolis: University of Minnesota Press, 2000.

Cain, James M. *Mildred Pierce.* New York: Vintage Books, 1989.

Cixous, Hélène, trans. Keith Cohen and Paula Cohen. "The Laugh of the Medusa." *Signs,* Vol. 1, No. 4 (Summer 1976), pp. 875-893.

Faber, Nancy. "A POW's Marriage Ends Bitterly." *People Magazine*, April 1, 1974.

Goode, James. *The Making of The Misfits*. New York: Limelight Editions, 1986.

Miller, Arthur. *Plays: Six*. London: Methuen Drama, 2009.

Spoto, Donald. *Marilyn Monroe: The Biography*. New York: Cooper Square Press, 2001.

Acknowledgments

The following essays were previously published, in slightly different form, in the following online outlets:

"Staying Clean" at Medium.com, December 2022.

"Bright White American Smile" as "Singin' in the Rain" in wig-wag, August 2020.

"Underside" in *Rivet,* November 2017.

"The Girl on the Bike" in *The Rumpus,* February 2017.

My gratitude to:

Michael Wheaton.

Everyone at Autofocus.

Henry Hoke. Elizabeth Gonzalez James. David Shields. Gabriel Blackwell.

Lucas Bailor. Daniel Elder. Alyson Evans. Julie Greicius. Kate Haake. Marissa Korbel. Neil Snowdon. Caren. Dr. Mishra.

Marisa Siegel and the Rumpus c. 2017. Brad Efford.

Andrew Gifford. Magdalen Rose.

All the directors. All of them.

Everyone who has supported my prior books: editors, reviewers, readers, retweeters, friends who asked and listened. I needed all of you to bring *Out There in the Dark* into the world.

Matt above all.

About the Author

Katharine Coldiron is the author of *Ceremonials*, *Junk Film*, and *Wire Mothers*. Her work as a book critic has appeared in the *Washington Post*, the *Guardian*, the *Times Literary Supplement*, and many other places; as an essayist, in *Conjunctions*, *Ms.*, *Booth*, and elsewhere. She and her books have been profiled in three countries on radio and television. Find her at kcoldiron.com.

— also from Autofocus Books —

Duplex — Mike Nagel

XO — Sara Rauch

Until It Feels Right — Emily Costa

Cleave — Holly Pelesky

Nextdoor in Colonialtown — Ryan Rivas

Too Much Tongue — Adrienne Marie Barrios & Leigh Chadwick

Picture Window — Danny Caine

the nature machine! — Tyler Gillespie

A Kind of In-Between — Aaron Burch

How to Write a Novel: An Anthology of 20 Craft Essays About Writing, None of Which Ever Mention Writing — ed. Aaron Burch

Hiraeth — Mistie Watkins

That Spell — Tate N. Oquendo

My Modest Blindness — Russell Brakefield

A Calendar Is A Snakeskin — Kristine Langley Mahler

Culdesac — Mike Nagel

Razed by TV Sets — Jason McCall

In the Away Time — Kristen E. Nelson

The Body Is A Temporary Gathering Place — Andrew Bertaina

Daughterhood — Emily Adrian

A Healthy Interest in the Lives of Others — Teresa Carmody

Leave: A Postpartum Account — Shayne Terry

Yes I Am Human I Know You Were Wondering — Erin Dorney

Organic Matter — E.N. Couturier

If I Can Be Honest: Selected Prose from the Four Years of Autofocus Lit (2020-2024) — ed. Michael Wheaton

www.ingramcontent.com/pod-product-compliance
Lightning Source LLC
LaVergne TN
LVHW051002080826
845145LV00009B/2420

* 9 7 8 1 9 5 7 3 9 2 3 7 0 *